Praise for *The Dog Wh*

"Dr. Dodman writes with sensitivity, ...
nary depth of understanding as he ...
This should be compulsory reading fo ...
—*ELIZABETH MARSHALL THOMAS, AUTH* ...

"Dr. Nicholas Dodman offers an entertaining and engaging account of common behavioral problems along with cutting-edge treatment ideas that will enlighten dog lovers everywhere."
—*JOHN J. RATEY, M.D., HARVARD MEDICAL SCHOOL, CO-AUTHOR OF* DRIVEN TO DISTRACTION *AND* ANSWERS TO DISTRACTION

"This is a brilliant book."
—*TEMPLE GRANDIN, PH.D., ASSISTANT PROFESSOR OF ANIMAL SCIENCE, COLORADO STATE UNIVERSITY, AND AUTHOR OF* THINKING IN PICTURES

"This is one of the best books for dog trainers and pet trainers to come along in years."
—LIBRARY JOURNAL

"An animal behavior book par excellence."
—KIRKUS REVIEWS

"*The Dog Who Loved Too Much* is about people who love a lot (can a person love too much?) and the wonderful objects of their affections. It is about a bond and a debt that is 140 centuries old. It is about caring enough to try to understand and the miraculous give and take of love."
—*ROGER CARAS, PRESIDENT OF ASPCA AND AUTHOR OF* ROGER CARAS' TREASURY OF GREAT DOG STORIES

"This is exciting reading [and] one of the most breezy, enjoyable books I have read on animal behavior in a long time."
—*JACQUE LYNN SCHULTZ, DIRECTOR ASPCA COMPANION ANIMAL SERVICES*

"A must read for anyone involved with dogs in any way. I read the book in just three sittings . . . and had to laugh and cry alternatively at the very familiar situations."
—KENNEL YELPS

"Dodman shares poignant, practical, and proven information on how to handle even the most frustrating behavioral problems."
—ARKANSAS DEMOCRAT-GAZETTE

The Dog Who Loved Too Much

Tales, Treatments, and the Psychology of Dogs

Nicholas H. Dodman, BVMS, MRCVS

BANTAM BOOKS

NEW YORK • TORONTO • LONDON • SYDNEY • AUCKLAND

THE DOG WHO LOVED TOO MUCH

A Bantam Book
PUBLISHING HISTORY
Bantam hardcover edition / April 1996
Bantam trade paperback edition / April 1997

ISBN 0-553-37526-1

Published simultaneously in the United States and Canada

Bantam Books are published by Bantam Books, a division of Random House, Inc. Its
trademark, consisting of the words "Bantam Books" and the portrayal of a rooster, is
Registered in U.S. Patent and Trademark Office and in other countries. Marca Registrada.
Bantam Books, 1540 Broadway, New York, New York 10036.

PRINTED IN THE UNITED STATES OF AMERICA

BVG 10 9 8

Dedication

To my wife, Linda, for her constant support
To my children, Stevie, Vicky, Keisha, and Danny—
for being there
To my mother for teaching me to care about animals

Acknowledgments

I would like to thank Bantam Books for giving me the opportunity to write this, my first book. I would also like to thank my two editors, Leslie Meredith and Brian Tart, who have so expertly steered me in the right direction with the final compilation. Their thoughts and ideas have been invaluable. Glen Hartley's initial enthusiasm and faith in the book has been greatly appreciated. Finally, I would like to thank author Joan Gage for her encouragement in the early days of this project, trainer Brian Kilcommons for his advice and support, and my assistant, Karen Hayes, for the wonderful job she has done in preparing the manuscript.

Several different pharmacologic agents are mentioned in this book for therapy of behavior problems in dogs. These drugs should only be prescribed by a licensed veterinarian who is familiar with their use. Drug doses vary considerably and side effects and idiosyncratic reactions may occur in some cases. In addition, many of the drugs referred to have not received formal (FDA) approval and a veterinary license. They may therefore only be prescribed when, in the veterinary clinician's opinion, they are truly indicated and when a veterinary label product that has the same action is not available. Also, the low protein diets referred to in the text should not be applied indiscriminately, especially in growing, pregnant, or nursing dogs. Veterinary advice should be sought before instituting such a dietary change.

Table of Contents

Introduction

M any years ago, before I had developed an interest in animal behavior, I was working in a busy practice in Glasgow, Scotland. One evening a man came into the
consulting room with a Jack Russell Terrier under his arm and tears
in his eyes. He shook his head slowly. "I'm afraid I'm going to have
to ask you to put her to sleep, Doctor," he said sadly as he gently
laid the dog on the exam table.

"What seems to be the problem?" I asked.

"Well, Sally here is very destructive. She attacks and eats the
phone whenever it rings. She has destroyed three phones so far,
and we just can't afford to keep replacing them."

"She eats phones?" I said incredulously. "Can't you just put the
phone out of the way?"

"No, I'm afraid not. She finds it wherever you put it. I love her very much and I haven't come to this decision lightly, but it looks as if we'll just have to put her to sleep."

I looked at Sally, who cocked her head slightly and looked back at me silently. She was a pretty dog and in her prime. It seemed such a pity to put her to sleep.

"Could I have one go at treating her?" I asked, dredging my memory for a solution to this problem.

"What would you do, Doctor?" the man asked.

"I could try putting her on Valium," I suggested as a long shot. "Maybe that would calm her down a little."

"All right," said the man. "It certainly seems to be worth a try."

I prescribed a relatively low dose of Valium to be given three times a day and sent the man home with his dog. The following week the man appeared again. He looked even sadder than before.

"It didn't work, Doctor," he said. "She has gone after the phones again. I'm afraid you're just going to have to put her to sleep."

"The dose I used was fairly conservative," I said. "Couldn't you give me another week and we'll try a higher dose?"

He agreed and set off again for another week at double the dose. The following week it was the same story—no improvement—and I knew I was running out of time. I pleaded for one last week at the maximum dose, and he agreed somewhat reluctantly to this final measure. When he finally returned after what seemed like an exceptionally long week, he was beaming from ear to ear.

"She's all right now, Doctor," he said. "I think we can keep her. Your medicine worked."

I was delighted at the good news and said to him, "So am I to understand she doesn't pay any attention to the phone at all now?"

"Well, no, that's not quite true," he said. "She still does try to get to it, but now she moves so slowly that I can catch her before she gets there."

This wasn't exactly the result that I had been looking for, but at least I had bought the dog some time. As it turns out, Sally finally gave up her pursuit of the phone, perhaps because she thought she would always be caught, and I'm happy to say she went on to live a normal life span.

Sally's case illustrates the dilemma that faced virtually all veterinarians twenty years ago: not knowing what to do when faced with a behavior problem. Most would simply refer the case to a local dog trainer and hope for the best. In some cases, this worked out well—but not always. Fortunately, veterinary knowledge of and interest in the treatment of behavior problems has burgeoned of late, and it is now one of the hottest new topics in veterinary medicine. Veterinary schools are developing animal behavior sections with faculty and resident trainees. Many veterinary students now have behavior courses as part of their curriculum, and continuing-education courses for practicing veterinarians often have animal behavior on their agenda. What this all means is that if you bring a dog with a behavior problem to your veterinarian, he or she either does or will soon have a good feel for what is going on and what to do. Already there are recognized specialists in animal behavior to refer difficult cases to.

Tufts University School of Veterinary Medicine, where I work, is one of the premier veterinary schools in the United States. We pride ourselves on being able to handle a plethora of conditions in all creatures, great and small. Because of this, we have established a well-staffed behavioral service in our hospital to help our clients deal with problem behaviors in their pets. We intend to learn and grow in this exciting new field and to assist in training present and future generations of veterinarians. Our program is not simply designed to deal with dogs that jump up or bark inappropriately, although we can and do handle these minor training-type problems. We are geared more toward the referral case, the more serious and refractory problems, with which others are less familiar. It is not unusual, for example, for us to find ourselves treating dogs that chase imaginary rabbits down imaginary rabbit holes, or swallow air until they swell up like weather balloons. Blanket sucking in the Dachshund, rage syndrome in Springer Spaniels, anxiety in Afghans, and obsessive-compulsive disorders (particularly in Golden Retrievers and Labradors) are also par for the course.

Trying to persuade some people to bring their pets in for an appointment sometimes presents a problem in itself. There is something about bringing a dog to a behaviorist that embarrasses owners, who are often very reluctant to ask for advice and afraid that they are somehow at fault. Sometimes families are divided about the necessity for an appointment with a behaviorist. Women are often more open in this regard. Men seem to feel that a trip to "the animal psychologist" is something wimpy, and are afraid to tell their friends for fear of being ridiculed. The uninitiated may have vague images of a voodoo-style veterinary psychiatrist who will put their dog on a couch and inquire about its puppyhood. Some owners even fear being psychoanalyzed themselves.

Clients are always relieved to discover that the consultation involves nothing more exotic than *making a diagnosis* based on clinical observation, a history, and sometimes laboratory tests, and then *giving treatment advice* to help correct the problem. They are also relieved to discover that treatment does not involve hours of training every day or any major changes in lifestyle. The sort of thing we advise involves changes in the pet's exercise, diet, and environment, a modicum of retraining (five to ten minutes twice a day), and specific behavior-modification therapy. The most important part of the consultation is educating owners about their pet's behavior. Many of the behaviors perceived as problems by the owners involve normal, species-typical behavior, on the part of both the animal and the owner, that isn't working out well in terms of the human–companion animal bond. In most cases, simply understanding the behavior, and what does and doesn't work in the way of treatment, is enough to put owners on the right track.

Aside from owner skepticism about the method and value of behavioral consultations, another factor that sometimes complicates case management is the owner's personality type and behavior. Owners may unwittingly contribute to their dogs' behavioral problem by sending them the wrong messages. For example, kindly, compliant owners can act as facilitators for dominant dogs, paying too much attention to the animals' likes and dislikes and not setting limits or expecting anything in return. (Some of these people also seem to have trouble managing their teenage children, and end up in a very similar situation with them!). A preliminary study we conducted here at Tufts indicated that the owners of dominant, aggressive dogs tend to have personalities that lean more toward the emotional than the rational. Understanding this has important implications in terms of treatment. Fearfulness is another condition that may be facilitated by owners' reactions. Anxious owners may transmit their own anxiety to their dog by their body language, tone of voice, and physical cues such as tensing up and tightening their hold on the lead during walks. All these reactions send a message to the dog that something is wrong. To make matters worse, these owners often then praise their dogs, rewarding the fearful response that they have just created. There are many examples of how owners' personalities can influence their dog's behavior, but none is quite so impressive as the codependent situation that develops between a needy owner and a dog with separation anxiety (the dog who loves too much). These owners are often extremely kind and thoughtful individuals who, perhaps because of some psychological need of their own, provide an inordinate amount of attention to their needy pet. Although it is the last thing they would want, these caring people actually worsen their dog's behavior problem. Part of the treatment plan for this and other behavior problems involves restructuring the relationship between owners and their pets so that, for example, the owner of the dominant dog knows how to set limits and be assertive; the owner of the fearful dog knows how to radiate confidence; and the owner of the dog suffering from separation anxiety knows how to train the animal to be independent.

One last area where owner personality can be of significance in treating behavior problems is in carrying out the treatment program. I have investigated the role of this only in the treatment of dominance-related aggression, where individuals who are more rational seem to be not only less likely to be the recipients of such aggression, but also more likely to be able to conduct treatment programs effectively when appropriately advised. Owner personality may be a factor in implementing behavior-modification programs for other conditions too. The ability to view a behavior problem objectively, and the commitment and tenacity to follow through with the treatment, are essential for good results to be achieved. One of the most common causes for the failure of behavioral programs is a lack of owner compliance. Many a good program has been wrecked for lack of this essential ingredient.

There is one area of behavioral therapy that sticks in the throat of individuals even after they have run the gauntlet of daring to tell friends and family about their prospective visit to the behaviorist and have finally summoned enough courage to make an appointment. I am referring to the use of medication to assist in the management of behavior problems. Although this has been done for years in a crude sort of way, recently modern psychoactive drugs have earned a place on the behaviorist's shelf. The use of these medications seems to imply that animals have a psyche (which, of course, they do) and that they're prone to mental disturbances similar to the ones that affect people (which they are). There are many parallels that can be drawn between the problem behaviors exhibited by dogs and equivalent behaviors exhibited by human beings. In fact, many behavior problems in animals are now being seriously considered for further study as relevant models of human psychiatric disease.

I was recently approached by a psychiatric researcher from Harvard who wished to study the genetics of canine aggression in the hope that this might shed more light on the inheritance of aggressive behavior in humans. It has been suggested as well that we could learn a good deal about panic attacks and anxiety disorders in humans from a more careful study of canine separation anxiety. There are also many similarities between compulsive behaviors exhibited by dogs, such as self-licking or ball playing or tail chasing, and human obsessive-compulsive disorder. To the uninitiated, these parallels may seem far-fetched. After all, a dog is a dog and a human is a human, right? Granted, there are many differences, but the biological similarities are striking. For example, the brains of dogs and humans are quite similar in structure and function. Even the same anatomical terms are used to describe the various brain regions in the two different species. Chemical messengers (neurotransmitters) are also identical in the two species and have similar functions, such as mediating mood, social behaviors, and sexual behaviors, although we are programmed a little differently in terms of our innate drives. It is hardly surprising, then, that similar things can go wrong with humans and dogs or that similar medications can be used for treatment of these problems.

The use of Prozac to treat compulsive disorders and aggression in dogs recently raised a furor. How could a human psychiatric medication be used to treat a dumb animal? Dogs don't get depressed or anxious, do they? Well, actually they do . . . and in general they experience a gamut of psychological problems similar to those of humans. Although early ethologists gave little credence to animal cognition, the current trend is to accept that higher animals do have a conscious awareness and can experience thoughts and emotions similar to our own. Much to the disappointment of the old school, Prozac and other psychotropic medications can be used quite effectively for the treatment of many veterinary behavioral problems. Antiobsessional drugs, tricyclic antidepressants, and various state-of-the-art anxiety-alleviating medications are proving invaluable in veterinary behavioral medicine. In most cases, though, they are best used in conjunction with specific behavior-modification therapy.

The conditions referred to in this book will be discussed with reference to real cases presented at our clinic (although the cases are real, to protect privacy, the names and identifying details for the people, and the dogs, have been changed), since a case-based presentation is more interesting and meaningful and helps the reader to understand and remember the conditions better. Although I trust that readers will find the stories entertaining, the transfer of information about the cause and treatment of canine behavior problems is my primary goal. There is more to canine behavior than meets the eye: There are good reasons why dogs do what they do, and in many cases there is a good chance that something can be done to correct the unwanted behavior. There is one caveat, however, for the unsuspecting reader. Not all the cases I describe have an entirely satisfactory conclusion, and some owners ultimately elected to put their dogs to sleep. *Euthanasia,* which has the literal if oxymoronic meaning "good death," is the word used to describe this ultimate solution, which behaviorists strive to avoid. Some of these sad cases are recounted here because they are a genuine but unfortunate part of behaviorists' experience. They highlight the urgent need for ethical dog breeding and the necessity of providing a suitable environment for our pets and utilizing appropriate management practices. It has been estimated that between 30 and 50 percent of dogs put to sleep meet their end in the nation's shelters or pounds. Sadly, unwanted behavior is the reason for the surrender of 20 to 30 percent of these dogs, accounting for some 1.5 million of the dogs euthanized annually. To put this into perspective, about three times as many dogs are destroyed because they have behavior problems as die from cancer. From a veterinary perspective, this is a large-scale problem and one that demands immediate attention.

The first section of the book deals with canine aggression: how it manifests itself, its types, and methods of treatment. Aggression is so widespread throughout the animal kingdom that it is considered by ethologists to be a normal phenomenon. For this reason (and for political reasons), aggression by itself is not defined as a psychiatric condition in humans, although it is considered a symptom of many psychiatric conditions. In veterinary behavioral medicine, we are a little more honest and accept aggression as a primary diagnosis.

Admittedly, many dogs that are diagnosed with aggression are simply showing extremes of normal behavior, but when the behavior starts to interfere with what should be a harmonious relationship between the pet and its owner or between the pet and other people or animals, there is, by definition, a problem. Aggression is the most common behavior problem reported in dogs. The most frequently encountered types are dominance-related aggression, fear-related aggression, and territorial aggression, although other types, such as pain-induced aggression and maternal aggression, come up from time to time. In this book, I will deal with the aforementioned "big three" aggression syndromes, and will also discuss rage syndrome (which is a pathological form of aggression), intraspecies (dog-on-dog) aggression, and the mixed causes of aggression that can create problems between dogs and babies.

The second section of the book deals with anxiety and fear-related conditions, such as fear of certain sights, sounds, or situations. A chapter is devoted to each of the common syndromes of separation anxiety and thunderstorm phobia. Separation anxiety is a condition that, as pitiful as it is, is relatively easy to treat—and treatment doesn't involve any yelling or belated punishment of dogs that have damaged property in their owner's absence. There is no reliable treatment for thunderstorm phobia, although I have some new thories about what's going on and feel I can make a lot of these dogs somewhat less apprehensive during storms. Another chapter in this section deals with some more unusual fears, such as fear of microblinds, fear of Thursdays, and fear of smells. Some of these true accounts provide insight into the way dogs develop fears and how they sometimes make irrational associations.

The last section of the book deals with that peculiar group of conditions known as compulsive behaviors and includes a chapter on canine acral lick dermatitis (lick granuloma), thought to be the nearest animal equivalent of human obsessive-compulsive disorder. There is also a chapter on my friends the Bull Terriers, some of which appear to obsess about certain toys or even their own tails to the point of being undistractable. These may seem like minor problems, but in fact they are not minor, and some can even be life-threatening. The final chapter in this section deals with the all-too-common problem of house soiling, including anxiety-related and fear-related reasons for this behavior. As will become apparent, the more difficult a condition is to treat, the more challenging I find it. I have made it a personal goal to find out what's going wrong in such cases so that they can be treated more effectively in the future.

I don't believe there are many dog owners who will fail to recognize facets of their own dog's behavior described somewhere in these pages. Recognizing the early signs of a problem and knowing what to do (and where to go) to prevent it from developing into something serious is invaluable. Exasperated owners who have been tolerating unwanted behaviors from their dog for too long will probably find help and advice somewhere in this book. Some may be able to make substantial improvements in their dog's behavior simply as a result of understanding their dog better. Since forty-two percent of dog owners report that their dogs have a behavior problem of one sort or another, and the shelters and pounds are busier than anyone would like to see, I hope that this book will in some way assist people and help them with their dogs. Dogs are, after all, man's best friend. The least we can do is try to understand them a little better.

PART I

The Aggressive Dog

CHAPTER 1

Leader of the Pack

I t was too good a day to be seeing patients. The pale spring sunshine that streamed from the cloudless New England sky invited outdoor activities such as yard work or a visit to the park with my kids. But I was in my office, and my pager buzzed quietly, interrupting my daydream and summoning me to a consultation. I picked up the case file, donned my white coat, and then hurried to the waiting room. Calling out the owners' name, I waited to see which of the many heads would turn. A young couple, who had been sitting at the far side of the waiting room gazing out the window, rose to their feet and turned toward me.

"Hi," I said cheerfully. "I'm Dr. Dodman. You must be the Scolettis."

"I'm Maria Scoletti," the young woman volunteered, a little

sheepishly, "and this is my friend Tony. We're co-owners of the dog."

I knew what they were going through. It's awkward enough to muster up the nerve to visit a "dog psychologist" against the better advice of your friends without having to stand up in public and advertise your personal arrangements. The whole thing seemed rather embarrassing for them. I glanced down at their good-sized juvenile Rottweiler. He was wearing a spectacular chrome-plated studded collar and was straining at his leash. The dog looked friendly enough. He radiated the energy and enthusiasm of puppyhood, though he was almost an adult in size and bulk. As we wandered toward the consulting room, Maria told me that he was eight and a half months old and had recently been neutered. We took our seats in the consulting room, me on my side of the desk and they on theirs; Rocky confidently sniffed around his new environment without a hint of trepidation.

My consulting room is set up differently from other veterinary consulting rooms to create a semiformal atmosphere and, I hope, to put clients at ease. I have no stainless-steel examination table or other tools of the trade, such as blood pressure cuffs, ophthalmoscopes, or otoscopes. Instead, there are spider plants and aloe, various behavior books, and fairly innocuous training paraphernalia, such as dog halters and leads. A couple of animal posters, a child's drawing of a Dalmatian, and a rack of brightly colored pamphlets on behavior issues decorate the walls.

Just looking at Rocky and the nervous couple, I had a feeling what their problem was going to be.

"So what's up with Rocky?" I ventured.

"He's biting me," said Maria.

"He bites only her," Tony hastened to add.

Now I was on the trail. This was probably a case of dominance-related aggression, sometimes colloquially referred to as the "yuppie puppy syndrome." In order to characterize the problem in Rocky, I proceeded to ask a long series of detailed questions about the situations that inspired aggression in the dog, and his daily activities, exercise (or lack of it), level of training, diet, manner of feeding, access to toys, games played, and demands for petting.

During the question-and-answer session that ensued, it also became obvious that Maria was much more relaxed and open than Tony. Women, I find, don't regard the behavioral interview as an indication of personal weakness or failure but merely as an information-gathering exercise. Men, on the other hand, often appear awkward and uncomfortable, even a little threatened. Their very presence in the consulting room, therefore, may indicate to me that they consider the problem to be extremely serious, and that they have a very close bond with the pet. Tony conformed to the stereotype. He sat anxiously in his chair, visibly tense with tightly clenched fists and jaw muscles. What would his friends think about his visiting a dog psychologist? I bet he didn't tell any of them.

Maria told me that Rocky got very little exercise, perhaps a one-mile walk each day. He ate the canine equivalent of rocket fuel, was obedient only about 70 percent of the time, and growled and snapped or bit in a number of different circumstances. On two occasions he had punctured her hand and drawn blood. The growling usually happened when Rocky was approached while eating or when in possession of a stolen object. It used to occur when Maria tried to lift him up. Luckily for her, this was no longer possible. More recently he had started growling while she was petting him, even if he had initially solicited this attention. Wiping his face or mouth was another activity that elicited an aggressive response. In addition, he growled when Maria attempted to touch his collar or put on his leash, or when she walked by him or talked to him while he was resting. This was especially likely if his lordship was disturbed by Maria while he was resting in a favorite spot on the couch. Once Tony had told Maria to show Rocky who was boss by hitting him with a newspaper. To their surprise, Rocky escalated his aggression by jumping up and snapping in her face. Why did Maria have all this trouble while Tony did not? The couple had no answers and no effective solutions to their problem.

At this point, Tony was becoming more relaxed and starting to join in the dialogue. This was good, since I knew he would have to buy into the treatment program if it was to be successful. I reassured them both that neither of them was to blame for their predicament. The condition had a name, dominance-related aggression, and probably had a genetic basis. It was most often encountered in males and in purebred dogs, and was well recognized in Rottweilers. Both Maria and Tony were relieved by the objective nature of the diagnosis.

My next job was to explain fully what was meant by the term *dominance*. Dominance is not some pathological state but rather a natural behavioral trait. A somewhat oversimplified view of dominance is to regard it as "the law of the pack": the driving force determining a hierarchy, ranging from the top dog to the underdog. When the hierarchy is stable, fighting is minimal and peace reigns; biologically speaking, energy is conserved by this arrangement. Convention dictates that individual members of the pack are assigned letters of the Greek alphabet ranging from alpha (top dog) to omega (underdog) to denote their pack standing. Although this analogy has some merit in transmitting an essential message to dog owners, in fact the real-life situation is more complicated, involving occasional role reversals in dominant-subordinate pairs. Even the omega dog when in possession of food may growl menacingly at the alpha dog, which in this situation, will often defer. After all, possession is nine tenths of the law.

Some researchers think that the dog pack is controlled not from the top but from within, possibly by middle-ranking females. This arrangement is termed a subordinance hierarchy. Certainly this type of organization occurs in other groups of animals, such as primates. In the early days, when scientists were first studying primate ethology, they would direct their attention to the most florid member of the group, that is, the largest and most vocal of the males, which appeared to be leading the group. More careful observation by recent researchers shows that although the apparently dominant male might make a lot of fuss and noise in attempting to lead the group, he would always glance furtively over his shoulder for acknowledgment by the real decision-makers of the group, the middle-ranking females. If thwarted by them in an attempt to initiate an action, the male would then inspect his fingernails or suddenly pay great attention to an imaginary flea while rapidly reorganizing his thoughts to come up with some better, more widely acceptable suggestion, rather than lose face. Finally, when his direction coincided with their inclination, the whole group would act, seemingly as a result of his initiative. The male would credit himself with having thought of the plan, thus preserving his self-respect, and the females would get their own way. Some think the canine pack may be organized something like this, but regarding it as a linear hierarchy seems to work when planning treatment strategies.

I explained to Tony and Maria that from Rocky's perspective, Tony was almost certainly number one, Rocky himself was number two, and, sadly, Maria was number three. The objective of our treatment would be to help them change the hierarchy to make Rocky subordinate to both of them. So that they didn't feel too sorry for him, I explained that dogs, unlike some humans, do not have to be number one. They are happy to be either second or third, or even lower, in a social hierarchy, but it is important for them to know where they stand. Sometimes dogs seem almost relieved when they find out that someone other than themselves is in charge, relieving them of unnecessary responsibility. Then the dog can simply get on with being a dog and leave the rest to the owners.

Of course, it can be hard to persuade a dominant dog that you are in charge, but that's the only solution to the problem. Older, now outdated, methods of getting this message across involved confronting the dog physically, meeting violence with violence. It was thought that if this tactic was started at an early age, it would send a clear message to the dog about who was in charge. Techniques such as lifting the dog up by its jowls, rolling the dog onto its back (alpha rolling), and staring into its eyes have been, and are still, used. To my mind, these methods are inappropriate, unnecessary, and in some cases inhumane. In any case, they cannot be performed safely with a larger dog. More extreme techniques such as hanging the dog by the lead and "the helicopter" (whirling the dog around in circles by the lead) have been reported to me by clients. Some people have even tried biting their dog! These techniques are totally inhumane and usually ineffective.

The best approach is to regard the dog as a child. Positive reinforcement of desired behaviors is the rule. You should not expect too much too soon, and you should ignore, or at least not respond to, unwanted behavior. If intervention is necessary, it should be nonconfrontational and should provide new direction. In other words, give the dog something to do other than what it is doing at the time. Yelling "No" is usually ineffective, and physical punishment should never be necessary.

Just imagine how you would view it if a physician recommended to you that you punch your child in the face to prevent some unwanted behavior. For most of us, this would not ride well. Yet some trainers will teach dog owners to stand on their dog's toes or knee it in the chest to prevent jumping up, spray it in the face with lemon juice to prevent barking, and use harsh choke-chain corrections to punish other unwanted behaviors. You could never train a circus pony or dolphin to perform using a choke chain or by means of punishment. In these animals the whole process is accomplished by positive reinforcement of serial approximations to the desired behavior—a technique called behavioral shaping.

I explained to Tony and Maria that training by positive reinforcement is an important aspect of gaining the psychological upper hand over a dog with dominance-related aggression and should be incorporated into their daily routine. Maria needed to work at having Rocky obey her consistently and quickly, initially when there were no distractions around. I explained that although dominant dogs do well in conventional dog-training schools, they do not generally bring their new-found manners home, and dominance-related problems usually persist. They will obey commands perhaps 70 percent of the time and only when they feel like it. When you really need them to do something, however, they just ignore you.

Even when dominant dogs do obey a command, they do it in a desultory way. "Down," meaning lie down on the floor, is the hardest command for the dominant dog to follow without some kind of resistance or revolt. Typically the dominant dog will spend a few long seconds gazing at the owner who has just issued the command "Down." He may then slowly go down onto one elbow, then the other, leaving his rear end sticking up in the air. Then, for an instant, he might dip and touch his chest on the floor before springing up and running around like an idiot, anticipating all kinds of praise and affection from the all-too-grateful owner. Alternatively, the dog may just look at the owner as though he had three heads. If the owner starts to shout and scream at the dog, the animal will either enjoy the show or retaliate with an aggressive warning.

For Tony and Maria, five- or ten-minute training sessions twice a day would go a long way toward reestablishing control. In these sessions, which should be fun for them and Rocky, I advised them to use one-word commands, such as "Come," "Sit," and "Down," rewarding a timely and accurate response with immediate warm praise and perhaps brief petting directed to Rocky's chest area. Commands were never to be repeated, and failed responses were to be ignored. I recommended that the training should at first be performed by Tony with Maria in attendance, but later should be performed by Maria with Tony nearby for support. Apart from advice on training, another essential piece of information that I transmitted to the pair, with Maria in mind particularly, was that they should avoid any confrontations with the dog. If, for example, Maria found herself in the presence of the growling Rocky misguidedly guarding his food bowl or resting place, she should, without any visible display of emotion, circumnavigate the area and busy herself with some other activity, not looking at Rocky, not speaking to him, and basically totally ignoring him. This technique alone would defuse the situation while we initiated a program designed to increase Maria's authority over Rocky.

Avoiding confrontation also serves to prevent further reinforcement of the aggressive response in these situations, and sets the stage for the extinction of the response. The next task for me was to explain why some circumstances could lead to aggression from Rocky, so that potentially dangerous situations could be avoided. Not the least of my goals was to show Tony and Maria Rocky's underlying motivation for what they had previously believed were unpredictable, unprovoked, and irrational responses.

Dominance is a behavioral trait designed to insure survival of the individual (and, therefore, the species). It is expressed in two main ways—competition over resources and self-protection. Competition over resources, sometimes termed possessiveness, can break out over food, valued objects (toys), cherished resting areas, and sometimes certain people of whom the dog is particularly fond. The second component of dominance, self-protectiveness, may be a response to threatening postures or gestures, such as bending over the dog and patting it on the head. If you try to make dominant dogs do something they don't want to do, they may come back at you with a growl or snap (or worse), and if you admonish them, the situation can escalate. Such dogs are the canine equivalent of willful, overindulged teenagers. They will do what you want them to do only when they feel like it. When they are not in the mood, forget it. These dogs need relatively less affection than their more submissive counterparts, and they also need their space. It is interesting to note that violent human criminals also need their space. The term *body buffer zones* has been coined to describe the physical space people like to have around them; in aggressive individuals, any intrusion upon this space induces a sense of uneasiness or threat. The more violent the criminal, the larger the body buffer zone. I told Tony and Maria that Rocky's aggression around food or stolen objects or when approached on the couch reflected the competitive or possessive components of his aggression. Self-protective components of his trait came out when Maria attempted to discipline him or otherwise physically deal with him.

In the wild, dominant dogs both initiate and terminate many activities that involve other pack members. It is reasonable, then, to expect the same type of behavior in relation to human pack members. Rocky would demand to be petted by Maria and then either walk off, leaving her hand suspended in midair, or growl to tell her that enough was enough. I asked if Rocky ever brought toys to her to be played with. She said he did and that when he was through he would walk off and leave her standing there. Par for the course. When retrieving a thrown tennis ball or Frisbee, he would stop eight feet short and insist that Maria come to him if she wanted to continue the game. Such behavior is the canine equivalent of one-upmanship, and it has to be combatted.

I advised Maria and Tony to put all Rocky's toys away and to provide these playthings only after he obeyed a command. Playthings that had previously stimulated aggression or very high emotions should be taken away forever. From that point on, all games should be initiated by Maria or Tony, not by Rocky. They should call Rocky to them ("Rocky, come. Good boy"), have him sit, and then throw the ball. They should terminate all games, too, by issuing a command such as "Cease" or "Enough," so that the game is over at their direction—even if they have to motivate the dog to make that final retrieval. Rough games such as slap boxing, wrestling, and tug-of-war were entirely forbidden. This caused Tony to wince, for, as it turned out, wrestling with Rocky was his favorite pastime. I stressed the importance of his compliance with the "no wrestling" edict by referring to the fact that German Shepherds and Rottweilers are prepared for protection work using tug-of-war tactics. Such dogs are trained to attack, wrestle, and pull at a padded sleeve, which ultimately is worn by a person who acts out the role of an escaping criminal. Prior to a competition, the dogs are riled up by showing them the sleeve and allowing them to attempt to wrestle it off the handler, amid much yelling and excitement. Tug-of-war also plays a valuable role in confidence-building for competition dogs.

One of the primary resources in a wild dog pack is food. Even if Maria and Tony were not having problems with Rocky around the food bowl, it would be important for them to show him that they were in charge of this valued resource. This is accomplished by requiring Rocky to work for every meal. He should be required to sit or lie down on command before having his food bowl put down in front of him. There should be no more free lunches! Once the food was down, Rocky should be allowed to eat undisturbed, but the food should be picked up after he has finished eating—but not before he has left the room, in order to avoid a confrontation. The point of picking up the food at the end of the meal is to make sure that he doesn't have the free choice to come back to the food later and eat. Some dogs are allowed to wander back and forth from the bowl, grabbing small bites throughout the day, as if it were a perpetual buffet. As far as dominant dogs are concerned, this does nothing to engender respect for the human food providers. If Rocky chose not to sit or lie down before a meal when instructed, he should simply not be fed that mealtime. That would send a pretty clear message.

Most owners are horrified to hear this latter advice. They think that their dogs, like them, require two to three square meals a day. This is completely false. Dogs are intermittent feeders in the wild. They eat only when they capture their prey. This sometimes infrequent event is followed by the dogs gorging themselves and lying around in a postprandial haze for hours before regrouping, socializing, and so on. The next day, the dominant pack member may organize another hunt, but there is no guarantee it will be successful. It is not uncommon for wild dogs to go forty-eight hours without a meal. Missing a meal would teach Rocky that Tony and Maria controlled the food resource and that they were prepared to deny it to him if he was foolish enough to disobey—a slightly Victorian attitude, but absolutely essential if they were to gain Rocky's respect.

Feeding should be instituted first by the most dominant member of the family. In Rocky's case, this was Tony. Once the ground rules are established, other pack members (Maria) can follow suit. In rare cases it may be necessary to begin by feeding the dog small quantities, requiring a positive response to a command prior to each helping to ensure a continued supply. Hand feeding, as dangerous as this might sound, can also generate great respect. When the feeding strategies are working well, the quality of the response can be improved. Tony and Maria were told that Rocky would initially be allowed three seconds to obey a command, but that as his proficiency improved the acceptable response time should be shortened to two seconds, then one second. Finally a virtually instantaneous response would be required. As petty as this may sound, it should be noted that it is in the nature of the dominant dog (and some churlish humans) to be purposely sluggish in response to any direction. In the British army this type of behavior is referred to as dumb insolence. Insisting on a rapid response to commands both at mealtime and during training sessions will instill greater reverence and respect in an unruly dog and, I suspect, from an indolent army private.

During the course of the dialogue I paused to make sure that Tony and Maria were still making sense of my advice and that it was practical for them. This is necessary in these interviews because the recommendations are something of a penance, and not every owner is able fully to comprehend or follow them. In this case, I felt my audience was with me, so with a clear conscience I moved on to another area, that of petting.

If done correctly, tactile stimulation of a dog—petting—is an extremely potent reward and, as such, is something that can be rationed by owners and provided only when a reward is due. Contrary to popular opinion, most dogs do not like to be patted on top of the head and, like us, don't like to have their fur ruffled. The best places to pet a dog are on the chest, under the chin, and behind the ears. The petting action that appears to be most appreciated is one of stroking or scratching. You will know when you are doing it right because your dog's eyelids may begin to close and he may get a far-off look. For some dogs, petting is ecstasy. Owners who pet dogs indiscriminately are, unbeknownst to themselves, rewarding their dog for nothing. This is not a problem if the dog is not dominant, but can undermine the authority of owners who find themselves losing control. Dogs that are petted for nothing have much less incentive to work for a reward. People are like this, too. If we received paychecks for not going to work, there would be no necessity to turn up every day, and many workplaces would be distinctly underpopulated. Powerful rewards should be paired with behaviors that the owners wish to promote.

"But he asks to be petted," exclaimed Maria. "Surely that makes him subservient to you."

Tony was on the ball.

"That's not right, Maria," Tony said, beginning to understand what I was saying. "He's not asking to be petted, he's *telling* you that you have to pet him, *right now.*"

"That is correct," I agreed.

"You mean all this time . . . ," said Maria.

I nodded at her sagely. "I'm afraid so."

It's not that I was forbidding the owners to pet their dog, although some behaviorists do—this is the so-called cold-shoulder approach. I was merely suggesting a strict rationing of this valued reward. Not only should Tony and Maria pet their dog only when he responds to a command, but they should also abbreviate the petting session and confine it to scratching him in the chest area or stroking his coat in the same direction that it grows (not roughing it up, as Granny used to do to our hair—which is just as objectionable for a dog as it is for a person).

The last key point that I wanted to make to them was that it was important to restrict Rocky's access to high places. It is generally observed that dominant dogs will be more aggressive when their eyeballs are on the same level as or higher than the family member's. This could occur if the owner is, for example, rolling around on the floor playing with the dog. I warned them, particularly Maria, about the danger of this. My senses had been sharpened to this type of interaction in a recent consultation regarding a dominant Lhasa Apso, which had all but removed his owner's nose during a wrestling session on the rug. The poor man had to have sixty stitches in his face, starting between his eyebrows and zigzagging across his nose into his upper lip. The other way a dog can physically raise his level with respect to the owner is by climbing up on top of something, whether it's a chair, bed, or sofa. Maria had already experienced considerable difficulties in this area, with Rocky's behavior ranging from a growl to a bite. So, from then on, high places were verboten.

"But how do you keep him off high places without getting into a confrontation?" Maria inquired, bringing up an excellent point.

"The first thing to do," I said, "is to try ordering him off the bed or sofa with a firm command such as 'Off,' said with feeling but not yelled." I went on to explain that if, by some chance, he jumped right off, then of course the correct response would be praise, warm praise from the heart, perhaps associated with one of those rare chest scratches, to make him feel very good about what he has done. If, however, he raised one eyebrow and sighed, remaining firmly in place, he should be called away (rather than hauled away) and redirected to some other activity, such as one that involves food, access to a favorite toy, or perhaps a walk outside. In either case, if he responded to a "Rocky, come. Good boy" sequence, he should be praised for obeying. Once again they will have achieved the desired response without confronting him. They will have simply directed him. If neither of these approaches worked, and if his high-place activities were confined to a particular location, then perhaps that chair or sofa could be made physically inaccessible by putting it away or tipping it up, or folding the pillows down when they weren't using it.

"Finally," I said, "the ultimate deterrent is upside-down mousetraps on the forbidden piece of furniture. These often do the trick and will, of course, work whether you're present or not. This teaches the dog that high places are not as pleasant as previously thought. A good trick is to cover the mousetraps with stiff brown paper so that when the dog jumps onto the couch or chair, the mousetraps snap against the paper with loud noises, causing the alarmed pet to leave the unpleasant scene in haste.

"You would probably only need to do this for a short while," I reassured Maria, "as dogs have excellent memories of adverse circumstances like this. And there is no way that he will be able to pin any of the blame on you."

The consultation was drawing to a close. I could see that Maria and Tony were still focused and intent, and judging from their smiles and nods, they were beginning to get a good feel for how they should deal with Rocky in the future. Rocky continued to promenade around the room, regarding me a little quizzically. Once he ventured to put his paws up on my desk, which I usually regard as the equivalent of the dog's signature on a piece of paper admitting to dominance. I had two more pieces of advice to offer before the couple departed with Rocky. The first concerned his level of daily exercise, or "output," as I termed it. Rocky had been getting a one-mile walk each day. We all agreed that for a strapping young male Rottweiler, this was a drop in the bucket. Twenty minutes of hard aerobic exercise every day was the bare minimum, I explained. "Basically," I told them, "a tired dog is a good dog!"

Turning to the input side, I also had a word with them about diet. It is widely held by trainers and behaviorists that certain diets will make aggressive or hyperactive dogs even worse. Nobody really knows why, but it is well known that diet can influence behavior in a number of species. Take horses, for example. If a horse on a high grain ration is brought into our hospital, for safety reasons, we generally don't allow students near the horse for a day or two, until it has come down from what amounts to a dietary high. Hyperactive children also may have their condition exacerbated by certain foods or food additives. In any event, many behaviorists believe that diet can significantly affect behavior. Some favor the theory that high amounts of protein increase activity and impulsivity. Others blame artificial preservatives, such as ethoxyquin, while yet another faction considers that dietary allergies may be involved somehow. I have anecdotal evidence to support each theory and some hard data supporting the use of low-protein diets to reduce territorial aggression in dogs, especially when fearfulness is a factor. To be safe, I usually recommend a low-protein, lamb-based diet that is free of artificial preservatives. Needless to say, this kind of food is somewhat unusual and cannot be purchased in supermarkets, so I direct owners to the local feed store or a specialized pet-supply store.

"Does this make sense?" I asked Maria and Tony. They seemed happy enough, nodding approvingly as they got ready for their departure. I handed them my printed notes on dominance with written instructions, which I suggested they attach to the refrigerator door. Follow-up calls were scheduled, and we sauntered out to the front desk, where they settled their bill. The interview had taken an hour and forty minutes and left me a little drained, but I felt that the job was well done. I thought that they would do well because they appeared to have understood the main message. Basically, Rocky now had to work for a living.

My optimism about Rocky's likely improvement was not unfounded, but neither was treatment success guaranteed. The outcome with all aggression cases must necessarily be guarded because there are so many factors that determine the subsequent course of events. Studies show that about two thirds of dominant dogs treated by the "nothing in life is free" approach improve considerably. Of the remainder, most are better than they were, but there is the occasional dog that fails to respond to this line of treatment. Why the difference, one might ask? A good question, and one that we are presently attempting to answer. Owner factors are almost certainly involved. Some colleagues and I have recently completed a study, using what is called the Keirsey Temperament Sorter, to find out which kinds of people wind up on the receiving end of a dominant dog's aggression and which of these is best able to cope when provided with the relevant information. What our results suggest is that dominant dogs may be more likely to show aggression if they are owned by more-sensitive, perhaps more-compliant owners. In addition, in our study there was a strong suggestion that pragmatic types of people were more capable of making improvements in their dog's behavior using a behavior-modification program such as the one recommended to Maria and Tony.

Whatever personality types Tony and Maria represented, it was imperative for them to work together to provide a unified front of resistance to their pet's willful ways. Unfortunately, the short-term outcome in Rocky's case was not as good as I had hoped for. There was only a 50 percent improvement at the two-month checkpoint, whereas I could reasonably have hoped for a 60 to 70 percent improvement at this stage. Tony had become delinquent in his responsibilities, and I was faced with what is euphemistically termed "failure of owner compliance." He felt that because he spent long hours away at work, when he came home he should be allowed to indulge the dog as he had before. This no doubt undermined Maria's authority, and the improvement was not as dramatic as it should have been. This wasn't the first case where people factors had interfered with a treatment program. Another dominant dog that was initially extremely resistant to treatment responded dramatically when a noncompliant and somewhat belligerent mother-in-law was relocated into her own apartment. Apparently she didn't believe in "this dog psychology nonsense" and simply refused to comply with the program, feeding and petting the dog at will. In this latter case, not only did the dog's behavior improve when the mother-in-law was rehoused but the family got on better, too, making for a happy ending all around.

I told Maria and Tony the mother-in-law parable and some other cautionary anecdotes, and launched them off again on their treatment program. This, plus weekly telephone checks on their progress, finally got them back on track, and they started to make headway again. Eventually Rocky improved to the point where he was not biting Maria and was no longer a danger to them. They had learned to deal with him using a nonconfrontational approach and were able to head him off at every turn. Of course, Rocky was still a dominant dog, and had to be managed that way, but the way he perceived the hierarchy within the home had been changed for the better as far as Maria and Tony were concerned—and probably as far as Rocky was concerned, too. Oftentimes it seems that wresting the control back from a dominant dog is viewed with relief by the dog. It's almost as if the dog is saying, "Thank heavens! For a moment there, I thought *I* was the one who was in charge."

Now there is new hope for people who have difficulty enforcing a treatment program for dominance-related aggression. It involves medication. This is not as Machiavellian as it first sounds, and it has a sound physiological basis. It has been discovered recently that a neurotransmitter called serotonin is instrumental in the creation and maintenance of dominant states, both in dogs and in humans. Dominance-related aggression is thought to be associated with fluctuating levels of serotonin. Because of this, serotonin-enhancing drugs have a profound antiaggressive effect, especially in dominance aggression. Although behavior-modification programs may also modify levels of neurotransmitters, they do so in a much less dramatic way than does medication. Drugs such as fluoxetine (Prozac), which increases serotonin levels, can be extremely effective at curtailing dominance-related aggression in some cases, enabling owners to quickly gain the upper hand. This permits frustrated owners to work more successfully with behavior-modification programs, and their early successes encourage their continued compliance with the program. Sometimes this pharmacological leg up is all that is needed to facilitate and encourage owner compliance and bring about successful resolution of a dominance problem. Although it is not necessary in all cases, pharmacological support of behavior-modification therapy has added a new dimension to the management of behavior problems and has dramatically increased the chances of treatment success.

I don't know that Maria and Tony would have gone for this line of treatment even if it had been available when I saw Rocky. Many people are averse to pharmacological treatment on moral or ethical grounds. Just the word *drug* is, to such individuals, like a red flag to a bull. Personally, I don't hold with this view and can address specific concerns one by one when necessary. I have found pharmacological therapy extremely useful as an adjunct in the treatment of dominance-related aggression and many other behavior problems, and believe that the timely and appropriate use of medications can save lives. It can only be hoped that those who elect to avoid medication for their pet when it is prescribed comprise the same group that conscientiously objects to euthanasia.

• TREATMENT FOR •

Signs of Dominance-Related Aggression

Aggression—growling, lifting a lip, snarling, snapping, or biting—directed primarily at family members or people with whom the dog is familiar, is often dominance-related aggression.

Situations Leading to Aggression

- *Competition*—overvalued resources—food, treats, bones, rawhides, stolen objects, resting place, bed, crate, owner
- *Postural challenges*—being hugged or petted, being patted on the head, being pulled back by the collar or the scruff of the neck, being stared at, being lifted up, grooming, nail trims
- *Being admonished or disciplined*—owner raises a finger or a rolled-up newspaper, hitting, yelling
- A *battle of wills*—trying to make the dog do something against its will

Treatment of Dominance

1. Adjust management—increase the dog's exercise and feed it a sensible diet (dog food only).
2. Fine-tune obedience training. Conduct five- to ten-minute sessions twice daily in a quiet environment. Make the sessions fun. Use one-word commands, give rewards for quick response, and ignore failed commands.
3. Make the dog earn all food, toys, games, attention, praise, petting, and freedom. For example, the dog must sit or lie down first—the canine equivalent of saying "please."
4. Avoid confrontations and do not use punishment.
5. Do not engage in rough play.
6. If prescribed, use medication (Prozac or Prozac-like drugs).

CHAPTER 2

The Jekyll-and-Hyde Syndrome

Not all kinds of aggression have a logical explanation, as dominance-related aggression does. Some are, frankly, pathological. Shortly after my initiation in clinical animal behavior, I heard the term *rage syndrome* used to describe sudden, violent, and inappropriate aggression shown by some dogs. You might think that all aggression is inappropriate, but this is really not so. In dominance-related encounters, it is natural for a higher-ranking dog to use the language of aggression to set limits on the behavior that it will tolerate from another individual. The form and intensity of the aggression is determined by the perceived gravity of the infringement. Predatory aggression, maternal aggression, and pain-induced aggression also involve innate mechanisms and are normal behaviors necessary for the survival of the individual and the species. Rage syndrome, also known as idiopathic canine aggression, is a term that is used to describe explosive, unprovoked aggression for which there is no apparent explanation. It is a type of aggression that is not even reminiscent of normal behavior, conjuring up images of a canine Jekyll and Hyde because of its intensity and unpredictability.

Dogs with rage syndrome may wake up from a deep sleep and immediately attack whatever is there—animate or inanimate. Other forms of aggression are not acted out like this. When owners of dominant dogs are questioned about the cause of attacks, they may say that their dog is aggressive "for no reason at all," but this is only how it appears to them. On questioning, it can usually be determined that the competitive or self-protective aspects of the dog's personality were aroused unwittingly. Although the events that trigger aggressive behavior may seem unimportant to us, they are not unimportant to the dog, which may not be in a mood to be trifled with in this way by a lower-ranking pack member. There is even a logical explanation for why fearful dogs bite or lunge at strangers or other dogs. The same cannot be said for rage syndrome, where even on close inspection, the initiating factor for the aggression is trivial, obscure, or indiscernible, even when the event is viewed from the behaviorist's perspective.

This aggression syndrome is thought to be most prevalent in certain breeds. English Springer Spaniels, in particular, have been singled out for special mention, and any extreme forms of aggression in this breed are, rightly or wrongly, branded as "Springer rage." Cocker Spaniels and Bull Terriers are two other breeds in which rage syndrome is thought to occur, but no breed has acquired such notoriety as the Springers when it comes to this syndrome. Interestingly, all three of the breeds mentioned are known for high levels of dominance, and there are certain lines of each breed that are thought to produce many dominant aggressive off-spring. The question is, where does dominance-related aggression stop and rage syndrome begin? There seems to be two schools of thought. One acknowledges the existence of rage syndrome but holds that it is so rare that even a busy behaviorist will see only one or two cases in a lifetime. Most cases of rage, this school believes, are in fact extremes of dominance-related aggression. The other school of thought has a much more liberal interpretation of what is meant by rage syndrome and basically includes in this category all forms of violent, uncontrolled canine aggression. This dichotomy of opinions will prevail until the condition can be more accurately defined. The question is, whether common or not, provoked or not, what is at the root of this extreme form of explosive aggression? The truth of the matter is that early in the study of canine behavior, nobody was in a position to support their opinion with facts. Some admitted this by using the label *idiopathic,* which literally means "of unknown cause." That was a fairly safe diagnosis. Others took a stance and attributed the condition to psychomotor epilepsy, basing their view on some rather inconsistent electroencephalographic evidence and the occasional treatment success using anticonvulsants such as phenobarbital. I wasn't quite sure what to believe and elected to shelve the matter until such time as the condition was presented to me for my own direct observation and evaluation.

In the early days of the Tufts behavior clinic, we were presented with an American Pit Bull Terrier that showed unaccountable paroxysmal aggression directed toward its owner. One of the most savage attacks was delivered while the owner was sitting at the kitchen table reading a newspaper, not looking at the dog and not moving a muscle. The attack was uncalled-for and savage. This is the type of history that raises suspicions of rage syndrome. Interestingly, this dog also showed some compulsive licking behavior directed at its left flank. I thought it was a bit of a long shot when a colleague I was co-consulting with tentatively diagnosed psychomotor epilepsy, but I went along with the diagnosis for the time being. Although I didn't hold out much hope of treatment success, I followed this dog's progress with interest. The first report was that the dog was doing "much better" on Valium, an anticonvulsant better known for its anxiety-reducing properties. This improvement was indeed encouraging, and my colleague switched the medication to phenobarbital, an anticonvulsant more appropriate for long-term management. Miracle of miracles, the dog stayed on course and maintained its improvement. Not only that, but the licking behavior ceased entirely. Our supposition was that the compulsive licking was somehow linked with partial seizure activity (the aggression) and that both behaviors were suppressed by the medication. This case focused my interest on seizure-based conditions, but on its own it didn't prove anything. There were all kinds of other explanations as to what might have been responsible for the improvement, including nonspecific drug effects such as sedation. Also, the owner may have been another innocent victim of the placebo effect, or may have simply told us what he thought we wanted to hear. We needed to treat more cases before we came to a firm conclusion.

During these early days, I had made some excellent contacts in the Boston area with people who were experts in all walks of behavioral life. One of these contacts, Dr. Klaus Miczek of the Department of Psychology at Tufts University in Medford, is known internationally for his elegant and original research on aggression. Miczek's methodology involves looking at aggression as an integrated response of an animal to its environment by observing colonies of animals in what amounts to a bioethological analysis. I was indeed lucky to have such an expert on aggression living on my back doorstep and even luckier to find that he was keen to cooperate and help shed light on some of the enigmas of clinical aggression in veterinary patients.

It was not long after my initial encounter with Miczek that I came across the first case that really warranted his involvement. The dog, called Randy, was an oversized, neutered male Chesapeake Bay Retriever weighing about 140 pounds. Randy's owner, Kathy Kirby, was a shortish, slightly built woman who weighed quite a bit less than Randy. The two of them together were a curious sight. Kathy had acquired Randy from a breeder when he was eight weeks old and had tolerated extreme aggression from him for five years, beginning when he was six months old. I gazed cautiously in Randy's direction as Kathy informed me about various spine-chilling aggressive incidents. Randy acted suspicious of me, lowering his head slightly and staring at me with hooded eyes from beneath his overgrown coat. I could almost guess what he was thinking: "Don't mess with me or I'll make hamburger out of you!" Aware of his great size and quickness, not to mention the thousand pounds per square inch of crushing force that he could generate with those jaws, I decided that discretion was the better part of valor and that any physical interaction with Randy should be attempted only if absolutely necessary—and preferably by someone else. Some of the incidents Kathy related smacked of dominance. For example, when he got a ball or towel, he would refuse to give it up and would growl menacingly and lunge at or bite anybody who he thought might be trying to rob him of his possession. He was also protective when it came to space and refused to permit anyone to pet or groom him. Nail trimming and discipline were definitely out of the question. Some of the other incidents, however, did not ring true in terms of straightforward dominance. Kathy reported that sometimes he would get in a really strange mood; when this happened, she said, he looked a little "out of it." At these times, he was at his most dangerous, and anything she did was likely to provoke a vicious attack on her. She couldn't walk around, she couldn't feed him, she couldn't leave the room; basically, she had to wait until the mood had passed before she could continue with her life. These mood changes would occur up to three times a day and last for the best part of an hour. Randy's aggression was not directed solely at Kathy. He would also attack inanimate objects, and had even crushed and swallowed wine glasses and ravaged a kiddy gate while incensed. When he was four years old, he attacked Kathy as she put a peach pit down the garbage disposal. She had her back to him at the time and didn't even see him coming. He knocked her down and bit her several times so badly that she had to be hospitalized. For some reason, Kathy was passionately fond of Randy, and parting with him was not an option for her, so I had to try to solve this problem. It was time to call in the reinforcements. I asked Dr. Miczek for a second opinion and made arrangements for him to visit the veterinary school to meet Kathy and Randy.

When the day came, I took Kathy and Randy to one of the neurology consulting rooms and had Kathy fill in some forms. I went back to the reception room and waited for Dr. Miczek. He arrived a few minutes late, beaming enthusiastically, and gave me a hearty handshake before we strode down the corridor to make our introductions. Dr. Miczek had never studied canine aggression, so this was a new experience for him, but I felt that together we might be able to make sense of Randy's bizarre aggressive behavior. He asked Kathy all sorts of questions about Randy and was obviously genuinely interested in the case. I noticed that he was particularly keen on finding out exactly what happened before and after an aggressive incident. He raised his eyebrows when Kathy related the mood change, but became even more animated when she described a sort of postaggression slump, when Randy became unresponsive to commands and oblivious to his surroundings. This, coupled with some subtle aspects of facial appearance (drooping eyelids and a slightly protruding tongue) and reports of Randy salivating during attacks, prompted Dr. Miczek to suggest a diagnosis.

"I think this could be a form of episodic dyscontrol syndrome," he said, seemingly expecting both of us to understand immediately what he was talking about.

We both looked at him for further clarification. He got the message and kindly explained the nature of the beast.

"Episodic dyscontrol," he said, "is a form of seizure-related aggression in which the patient has focal seizures confined to the temporal lobe of the brain. The centers that control emotion are housed here, so any disturbances in this region will cause significant mood changes associated with autonomic processes, such as salivation. Episodic dyscontrol has been used as a murder defense," he went on. "It is a highly controversial subject. After a murder, defendants sometimes claim that they must have suffered from a bout of the episodic dyscontrol syndrome in which they lost consciousness and control. In other words, they claim that they have a mental illness—and some of them may. The problem is episodic dyscontrol syndrome is almost impossible to substantiate. Some people believe that the aggression occurs only during a seizure. Others believe that the aggression is an interictal phenomenon—

that is, it occurs between seizures. Either way, diagnosis presents a problem."

Very interesting, I thought, but wouldn't we have the same problems confirming the diagnosis in a dog? I questioned Dr. Miczek about this, and he told me that he thought the best way to proceed was to have a veterinary neurologist perform a full clinical examination of the patient and then run an electroencephalogram, applying physiological challenges in an attempt to elicit the seizure activity. This was all set up very quickly, and our faculty neurologist, Dr. Hans Thalhammer, drew the short straw. I must admit, I was extremely impressed by his valor in dealing with the growling Randy. He simply scolded Randy for any particularly vocal outbursts and talked to him in a singsong voice as he examined him. During the course of the examination, Thalhammer flexed and extended Randy's paws, tapped his knee with a little rubber hammer, and palpated his spine, declaring ultimately that there was nothing noticeably wrong, barring the peculiar facial characteristics noted earlier. Kathy nervously agreed to allow us to give Randy an anesthetic in order to facilitate the electroencephalographic examination. She signed a consent form and then took a seat in the waiting room, leaving us to it.

I sedated Randy with a tranquilizer before inducing anesthesia with gas through a face mask. Dr. Thalhammer placed needle electrodes into Randy's scalp, and the nine or so pens on the electroencephalograph all started jiggling up and down on the rapidly moving recording paper, producing an image of the electrical activity occurring in Randy's brain. We didn't see much at first, although there was some excited discussion about the patterns that were emerging. None of them, however, was conclusive. Occasionally Dr. Miczek and Dr. Thalhammer, who were both of Teutonic descent, would lapse into German, leaving me incommunicado. Suddenly they would realize that I was still there, and one or the other would attempt to give me a summary of the preceding few minutes of conversation. Eventually we got around to applying the physiological challenges that Dr. Miczek had predicted would be necessary to unearth any abnormal activity. We decided on an auditory challenge first, using a clicking device or the sound of keys jingling right next to the dog's ear. Then came a visual challenge, which was provided by a strobe light generator, and finally we used a physical challenge, a toe pinch. During the application of these challenges, the EEG was monitored continuously and annotated to indicate the application and withdrawal of each stimulus. The real excitement arrived when the toe pinch was applied and a compound spike pattern was observed. I didn't know much at this time about interpreting the recordings, but Dr. Thalhammer was emphatic that this was an abnormal finding, and the handshaking and congratulating began.

While Randy was recovering from the anesthetic, I walked outside and explained to Kathy what we had found. The abnormal brain waves, I informed her, were located in the part of the brain responsible for controlling Randy's emotions and could account for his aberrant behavior. We suggested treating Randy with anticonvulsant medication, but told her there were no guarantees, so she should take extreme care to prevent any injury to herself or others in the weeks to come. The medication, I explained, was not a panacea, and in any case would take two or three weeks to reach its maximum effect.

I spoke to Kathy about ten days after the appointment, and she reported that Randy was doing much better. The aggressive attacks had lessened in both intensity and frequency. Subsequently Randy continued to improve, and Kathy was ecstatic. It was about this time, however, that she ran into some personal problems, and in the shuffle Randy's medication was omitted. He became aggressive again within days, and as soon as I heard what had occurred, I strongly suggested that Kathy reinstate the medication. This she did, and Randy improved once more and lived virtually free from serious aggressive incidents for the remainder of his days (which, as it happens, were numbered). I often think about Kathy and wonder how she tolerated all those years of physical assault and yet still loved that big hunk of a dog.

A short while after our confirmation of rage syndrome in Randy, my next canine suspect was delivered to the clinic. This case involved one of the more classically affected breeds, a Cocker Spaniel. Jody, as he was called, a parti-colored Cocker, had been a stray, and there was some reason to think that his aggression might have been fear-related. On careful inspection, though, the aggressive episodes were found to be heralded by a mood change, were often noted to be extremely violent in nature, and were followed by periods of inactivity and dissociation. There were also signs of activation of the autonomic nervous system during his vicious attacks. I decided to run an electroencephalogram on him and to apply the same challenges that we had applied to Randy. The abnormalities we detected on this recording were even more obvious, with multiple spikes and some oscillating activity termed spindling. Jody was diagnosed with episodic dyscontrol syndrome, was treated with phenobarbital, and was discharged. Within weeks he was 100 percent better, and even now, some years later, he is kept free of aggression by a single daily dose of phenobarbital. The owners know the medication is working because they have forgotten to give it on one or two occasions and Mr. Hyde has reemerged.

Hot on the heels of Jody came my first Springer, a three-and-a-half-year-old neutered male called Barclay. Barclay would get in a strange mood, attack violently after a trivial provocation such as someone walking by him, and then sleep for hours. (By contrast, dominant dogs seem to bounce back from aggressive incidents, seemingly becoming contrite or remorseful, or even appearing to be unaware of what has occurred.) Barclay was subjected to electroencephalographic examination, and once again the tracing was abnormal in response to our challenges. Barclay too was medicated with phenobarbital and was much improved, although he still had his moments. Every week or two he would get into one of his moods, particularly in the evening after he was fed. His owner was reluctant to increase his dose of phenobarbital, but had learned to work around him when the Mr. Hyde side of his personality took over, so an acceptable, though brittle, peace was achieved.

Other dogs with symptoms of rage syndrome have been brought to our clinic since Randy, Jody, and Barclay. Thanks to our new diagnostic method, we have been able to confirm the nature of the problem conclusively in each of them and to suggest a logical treatment. In general, the anticonvulsant treatment has been quite successful, but the response is not always as good as I hope for. I have, however, refined the anticonvulsant regime recently and often employ more than one drug simultaneously. This seems to help. Rage syndrome is not a typical animal behavior problem. It is the result of a physical problem, and is basically a form of localized epilepsy. It is very important for behaviorists to recognize these curveball diagnoses because no amount of exercise, dietary manipulation, or obedience work would ever help a dog with such a problem. The only solution for this type of problem is to encourage intelligent breeding of dogs and to treat affected individuals medically.

• TREATMENT FOR •

Signs of Seizure-Related Aggression

Violent, uncontrollable episodic aggression is elicited by a trivial stimulus. There is a pre-aggression mood change, which lasts for minutes or hours before an attack and a post-aggression depression with reduced responsiveness. It is sometimes associated with compulsive behaviors, such as self-licking and snapping at imaginary flies.

Diagnosis

- History of symptoms (breed may be significant, too)
- Neurological examination
- EEG (special technique is required for accurate confirmation)

Treatment

1. Exercise extreme caution in dealing with an affected dog, especially when it is behaving peculiarly.
2. Medicate with an anticonvulsant, such as phenobarbital.
3. Monitor the dog's behavior closely and be prepared to adjust the animal's medication and your interaction with the dog accordingly.

Seizure-based aggression, or episodic dyscontrol, is one of the few veterinary behavioral conditions in which euthanasia is a reasonable option because 100 percent cures are rare. Especially if there are young children in the household, it may be dangerous to keep the dog.

CHAPTER 3

Beware of the Dog

S ometime in the mid-1980s, shortly after our behavior clinic opened, I had cause to do some serious thinking about a condition referred to as territorial aggression. At first glance, the condition seemed quite elementary and easy to comprehend. After all, a dog's territory is the home area that it will actively defend against invaders, and aggression is the means by which this defense is accomplished. Case closed? Maybe not. The first sticking point for me was that most cases of "territorial" aggression reported to me involved aggression directed toward people—strangers—visiting the homestead. Ethologists normally describe territorial aggression as occurring between animals of the same species rather than as a cross-species phenomenon. From this standpoint, dog aggression to people visiting the home is a novel expression of this behavior. A classical example of territorial aggression can be seen in the avian world, where robins will defend their territory to the death if necessary . . . against other robins. Paradoxically, this behavior confers a survival advantage. But whoever heard of a robin defending its territory against assault by a lizard? Why should the robin care about lizards, since they don't compete for nesting sites, don't eat the same food, and don't share the same mates? The answer is that they really *don't* care. Why, then, should a dog actively defend its territory against people? Could it be that dogs view their human family as dog surrogates and therefore see visitors as competitors? Certainly dominant dogs appear to view their human family as members of their own pack. Perhaps the syndrome represents a sort of canine dyslexia, in which people and dogs have interchangeable roles. As some vindication of the role of territoriality in this type of aggression, I was able to thumb through a well-known veterinary behavioral textbook and find there, described in black and white, this very syndrome: "territorial aggression toward people." I noticed, however, that at the end of the paragraph the author noted that this was a "unique" expression of territorial aggression, leading me to believe that the author, like myself, had agonized over the definition.

During the course of routine behavior consultations, I have seen many dogs exhibiting what I will call territorial aggression directed toward people, and I have become familiar with the behavioral repertoire characteristic of the condition. Sheena, an extremely handsome eighty-pound German Shepherd who was brought to see me one December day, presented the classic signs of the problem. Sheena's owner, Sandra Rogers, an easygoing and affable young lady in her twenties, glided into the consulting room behind her dog and took a seat. Her eyes twinkled as she told me excitedly that she had learned about our behavior clinic on a television show.

It did me no end of good to hear her enthusiasm about our relatively new consulting service, and I listened with pride as Sheena and I eyed each other cautiously from opposite sides of the room. I glanced at some of the details on Sheena's record. Age of pet: two years and ten months. Sex: female. Reproductive status: neutered. Age when acquired: six weeks. I then surveyed the interactions between dog and owner. It was obvious that Sandra had a great deal of affection for Sheena, and I came to understand that the dog was a significant other in her life. She would glance at Sheena admiringly from time to time during the interview and would praise and pet her lavishly whenever she came within arm's length. There wasn't much doubt in my mind that Sheena had been spoiled, but I didn't think that dominance was going to be the problem here, for two reasons. First, I have only rarely had to treat a German Shepherd for dominance-related aggression, and second, Sheena's behavior in the consulting room was typically fearful. She moved timidly around the consulting room, nervously exploring the corners of the room farthest from me. Her ears were down and her tail was tucked as she walked with a crouching gait, pausing periodically behind Sandra and flashing me a sideways glance. After a brief pause, Sheena would resume her anxious patrolling, stopping now and then to investigate a strange odor, feigning indifference, but obviously cocked and loaded like a gun ready to go off. I employed my usual strategy of remaining seated and simply ignoring her. Eventually Sandra got around to telling me the reason they were there: Sheena's aggression to strangers.

On questioning, it emerged that Sheena's aggression was almost exclusively manifested in and around Sandra's home or in her car. Territorial right? Strangers coming to Sandra's home would elicit a ferocious display of barking and intimidation from Sheena. When confined in the house, Sheena would run back and forth from the door to the window, jumping on the furniture and peering out, as if she wanted to visually confirm the presence of the stranger she heard approaching. As usual with territorial aggression, uniformed visitors were prime targets, eliciting the most extreme displays of aggression, including lunging, growling, and baring of teeth. One has to feel sorry for these visitors, who—for no reason that they can fathom—suddenly find themselves in what seems to be a life-or-death situation. Individuals brave enough to enter the house were all right as long as they got seated quickly and remained seated, spoke quietly, and moved slowly. Suddenly reaching for the sugar bowl or getting up to go out, however, could elicit another outburst, especially, it seemed, if the individual was frightened of the dog. The episodes were worse in Sandra's presence and when the visitor's back was turned. This made leaving the house a pretty hair-raising experience. Although most dog owners interpret aggression to strangers as a protective, almost noble behavior, it is most likely driven by fear and represents a cheap shot from an insecure dog. These dogs have their confidence boosted by their owner's presence and are more courageous when their victim shows signs of fear or is turned away from them.

Sheena's aggression to visitors initially was noticed when she was only a few months old and was first considered a problem when she was six or seven months of age. Aggressive displays of this nature are often encouraged by people, especially men, who find it amusing in pups and justify it as a desirable guard dog trait. What they forget is that aggression increases with experience and grows with the dog. An eighty- or ninety-pound dog flying at the door when guests arrive is a totally different prospect from a puppy displaying the equivalent behavior. I don't know whether Sandra had indulged in any reinforcement of Sheena's aggression, but she ended up in the same predicament anyway. To some extent the behavior is self-reinforcing, as the consequences are reward enough. The development of aggression to the mail carrier provides just one example of how this can happen. He arrives every day to deliver mail, initially generating anxiety and causing protest barks from the young puppy. And what does our mail carrier do next? He leaves, of course! The dog connects its own barking with the mail carrier's departure as a cause-effect relationship. Inebriated with pride, taking credit for driving the bogeyman away, the dog will bark more confidently on subsequent days, and in time will completely master the art of intimidation. Snarling, lunging, and open-mouthed displays are gradually added to the repertoire. Of course, by this time the behavior has also generalized to include all uniformed visitors.

Aggression outside the house follows more or less the same pattern and, to the owner's surprise, often extends up and down the street and for some distance around the neighborhood, including neighbors' yards. This was the case with Sheena. She, like other canine culprits, was not aware of the legal boundaries of her owner's property, and as a rule of thumb (or dew claw?) regarded any regularly patrolled and urine-marked area as conferring the home-field advantage. Some say that territorial aggression outside the home can be reduced if you compel your dog to urinate on your property, not allowing it to stop at various locations around the neighborhood. This is supposed to limit the size of the marked territory and decrease the likelihood of aggressive encounters outside the owner's own yard. Whether this is true or not I cannot say for sure. Sheena herself had not been limited in this respect, and certainly could become aggressive even when she was some distance from Sandra's home. When she was in the yard, passersby, particularly joggers, skateboarders, or cyclists, caused her to run barking along the fence and engage in aggressive displays. The people invariably disappeared rapidly, leaving Sheena to wallow in the success of another accomplishment, further reinforcing the behavior.

Besides the house and its surround, Sheena's other prime site for aggression was the car. She would "protect" the car from any approaching individual, except Sandra, and her displays were quite violent and intimidating. I had Sandra put Sheena in her little red sports car and approached it myself to get a better feel for what I was dealing with. Sheena proved to be most intimidating, barking ferociously and hurling herself against the windows. Curiously, however, if the window was rolled down a few inches so that I could insert my arm inside the car, she would immediately stop barking and press herself against the opposite door. Perhaps she wasn't quite as brave as she looked. Then came the questions about the toll booth collector. Was Sheena a problem when Sandra picked up toll tickets or paid tolls? "You bet" was the unequivocal response. This was such a problem that she would often avoid toll roads and take an alternative route. I suspect that Sheena's reaction to toll booth collectors arose in very much the same way as aggression to the mail carrier and other uniformed visitors. That is, the toll collector came into view, Sheena barked and lunged, and then he disappeared. This is the canine equivalent of Caesar's *veni, vidi, vici*. So well had Sheena learned this routine that she was even beginning to apply it from within the moving car to strangers walking down the road. Approaching pedestrians would cause Sheena to throw herself barking from one side of the car to the other, pausing occasionally to snarl in the direction of the threat. All was calm once Sandra had driven on and the stranger was lost from view.

Having seen Sheena and heard the story, I confirmed in my mind once again that fear appeared to be a major component of this condition. Sheena was really a wimp and afraid of strangers. She had probably become this way, at least in part, because of her genetics, but this behavior was also due to improper socialization to people in a critical period of development, the first three months of life. Genetic influences are implicated because a large number of dogs with this condition are German Shepherds or other guarding or herding breeds. Improper socialization is also involved because environment plays such a major role in the development of fear responses, permitting dogs such as Sheena to learn that a good offense is the best defense. The reason for the apparent territorial nature of the problem is that dogs are more confident on their own pitch, including that extension of territory, the owner's car. When away from home and confronted by the same challenges, dogs with fear-driven territoriality show their true colors. In my consulting room, for example, Sheena initially appeared fearful and apprehensive, even though Sandra was there to lend support. I have no doubt that if I had first met Sheena in her own home, it would have been another story. By the time I got around to explaining all these things to Sandra, Sheena had fallen asleep and was snoozing peacefully on the floor at her feet (of course). Just then there came a knock at the door, and Sheena leaped to her feet, barking aggressively and baring her teeth. Whoever it was that was thinking of coming in, changed his mind. Good plan!

Before discussing Sheena's treatment with Sandra, I asked her another couple of questions for my own interest. The questions related to predatory aggression, which I had noticed seemed to be associated with the syndrome. Sure enough, Sheena was extremely motivated by squirrels, rabbits, and other small animals, which she would chase into oblivion, or until the prey found sanctuary up a tree or down a hole. Predatory aggression, whether by dogs or by other predatory animals, does not involve much affective display (snarling, baring of teeth, and so on) because for a hunter, grabbing a bite on the run is nothing to get bent out of shape about. In this instance, the lure is often small and furry and moving very fast. Some behaviorists believe that predatory instincts can be transferred onto modern prey, such as joggers, skateboarders, cyclists, or automobiles—basically anything that moves. Although this would fit in with behavioral observations of dogs such as Sheena, it is not easy to see why fear and predation should be linked. One explanation could be that sheep-herding dogs were engineered by us from ancestors with marked predatory drive to lack final commitment—that is, they were inhibited from performing the full bite and the kill. Sheepdogs who bite sheep don't last long in their jobs, and they are certainly not used for breeding. Along the same lines, it is interesting to note that untrained German Shepherd dogs are reluctant to bite hard, often tearing at clothing or only just puncturing the skin. When you consider what they are capable of, this implies a remarkable degree of self-restraint—or a lack of confidence. My vote is for the latter. Perhaps we are now in a better position than ever before to predict which types of dogs do have a bark that is worse than their bite!

A fundamental part of Sheena's treatment was to increase her exercise and take her off a high-performance ration, substituting a different diet for safety reasons. In addition, I advised Sandra to use extreme care when receiving visitors, either shutting Sheena away or using a muzzle. Specific behavior-modification therapy, in the form of a systematic desensitization with counterconditioning, was designed to reduce Sheena's fear and uncertainty with regard to strangers. Sandra was instructed to introduce Sheena to strangers in a gradual way, starting with those least likely to induce a fearful response and escalating to more severe challenges, and using distance as a variable factor. At first, the least threatening variety of person, in this case a woman, would be asked to stand in the street outside Sandra's home. Sheena, on lead, would then be walked out into the yard and instructed to sit and stay. Sandra was told to praise her warmly, pet her, and offer her a delicious food treat if she remained calm and composed. If Sheena refused to obey the command and paid unwanted attention to the stranger, the exercise would be repeated a few minutes later with the stranger at a greater distance. Successful completion of the exercise at one level would be grounds for escalating the challenge: having the stranger approach a few steps closer. Fine points of the program included varying the location of the training to include all points of access to the property and, eventually, to the house itself; never pressing Sheena to the point of a serious eruption of her behavior; always ending a training session on a positive note; and training as often as possible (at least two or three times weekly). In Sheena's case, training success with a few female volunteers would then lead to progression to the next level of challenge: men in plain clothes, starting with them on the street, as before. Ultimately, Sheena was to be desensitized to uniformed individuals as well, but this stage was some time off yet. Training Sheena to anticipate a pleasurable outcome of these staged encounters was to be centered on the use of praise, petting, and highly palatable food treats, such as bits of freeze-dried liver. The technique of teaching a dog to anticipate an outcome different from that previously ingrained is termed *counter-*

conditioning, and, if food reward is to be used, it works especially well if the dog is hungry. Desensitization programs, such as the one I described to Sandra, have their ups and downs, and they take time. I often tell people it is like playing a game of Chutes and Ladders. Sometimes you get a chute, slip back, and have to wait your turn to roll again, but on other days you may shift levels quickly and with great ease.

Finally, to assist Sandra with the desensitization exercises, I told her about a special halter she could use to help her gain good control of Sheena. The halter is designed with a nose band and neck strap, and signals to the dog that the person holding the lead is in control. The lead attaches under the dog's chin, so when tension is applied, it has the effect of closing the dog's mouth and simultaneously applying gentle pressure to the nape of the neck. Some say the signals delivered to the dog are similar to the ones that a bitch uses in controlling her pups, when she holds them by the muzzle or grabs them by the scruff of the neck. Whatever the explanation, the system seems to work well for many dogs. Without halters we would certainly be in trouble managing large animals such as horses and cows. An obstreperous horse could never be controlled properly with a rope or chain around its neck. It would simply drag the would-be controller along the street, as the neck is a relatively insensitive area. A halter applied to the head, however, will provide good control by applying pressure in appropriate and sensitive areas. The same principle applies when using a nose ring in a bull or a snout snare on a sow. It is little surprise that halters also work for dogs. Halters provide an effective and humane control system for dogs, and what's more, it doesn't take long to learn how to use them. Although most dogs take a few minutes to adjust to a halter and may try to scratch it off, once they have accepted it a halter works like magic, having an apparent placating effect and affording the owner exquisite control. After that, treatment relies on positive reinforcements, such as food treats, all the way.

Following the general discussion of desensitization with Sandra, I talked with her about the dreaded toll booth collectors specifically. I asked Sandra whether it would be possible for her to take Sheena to a toll booth a couple of times a week to desensitize her to the toll booth collectors. In addition, I asked Sandra to organize a little counterconditioning at the toll booth, by arranging to have some dog treats left at a particular window. That was it for our first session, and Sandra went on her way, halter in hand and Sheena at her side.

As time went by, Sheena improved. When strangers came to the house, she could be put into a sitting position next to Sandra and was obligated to stay there because of control affored by the halter. Sheena was then rewarded for good behavior, being given treats as guests arrived and entered the house. The important thing for Sandra to remember was to maintain control of Sheena and let her guests look after themselves. On entering the house, guests were informed to avoid looking at, approaching, speaking to, or touching Sheena, and to get seated as quickly as possible. They were also told to grab a handful of dog treats that had been conveniently placed in a bowl by the door. During the course of conversation, the guests were instructed to slide treats across the floor toward Sheena, and her satisfaction with the treats was construed as a positive sign. It was emphasized to Sandra that whatever transpired, it was important for visitors not to force themselves on Sheena but to wait for her to approach them. Sheena was on a long lead and was allowed to approach strangers in her own time (as long as things looked good). Any signs of balking were treated in a perfunctory manner, with Sandra simply instructing her to sit or lie down and then continuing with life as usual.

About three or four months after I first saw Sheena, Sandra reported that the retraining was going very well and that there was improvement in all areas except during car travel. Apparently Sheena would still bark her head off at people on the pavement as Sandra drove along, and this was beginning to be the most serious remnant of her previous behavior. Sandra was advised to keep the halter on Sheena in the car at all times and to thread the lead under the front seat so that she could maintain Sheena in a down position in the back of the car. She was advised to practice this with the car stationary before taking to the road, and was able to master this quite quickly. Sandra was also instructed in the noble art of using a shake can. A shake can is simply an empty soda can or beer can filled with ten to fifteen pennies and then taped shut. When it is shaken, the noise startles the dog into stopping whatever activity it is engaged in. I believe the pennies produce an ultra-high-frequency sound that is aversive for some dogs, so that the noise both distracts and punishes the dog. This type of device works much better for a fearful dog than for a dominant one. After an initial underreaction, dominant dogs often learn what is to transpire and take whatever action is necessary to prevent their owners from reaching for or shaking the can. Fearful dogs, on the other hand, may be controlled quite successfully providing the can is used in a discriminating way and for a specific purpose. Such was the advice to Sandra, and between the halter control system and the shake can, her problems with Sheena in the car were largely solved. It has now been a couple of years since I first saw Sheena, and the improvement has been sustained. Sheena is not perfect and never will be, but she is much more manageable than before. Sandra is a lot more confident with her new-found control, and her guests are a lot safer. Car travel continues to be peaceful and, thanks to the treats, even the toll booth collectors are smiling. Sheena still does a bit of barking when uniformed individuals approach the house and is none too keen about the telephone ringing, but she is certainly a lot better than she was.

Several months after I saw Sheena, I had a phone call from another German Shepherd owner, Brent Thomas. Brent was most distraught about the fact that the local authorities in his town had impounded his dog, Max, who for some weeks now had been on death row, awaiting execution. The alleged crime was that of attacking and biting neighborhood children on two occasions. On the first occasion, Max had slipped out of the garage and terrorized children in the street, chasing and barking at them. One of the children was bitten, though not severely, and ran home screaming to his mother. His mother alerted the local authorities, who impounded Max and only released him reluctantly, with strict warnings to Brent. On the second occasion, Max was free in the yard again, having successfully engineered his way out of the garage Houdini-style, when a hapless boy on a bicycle stacked all the odds against himself by taking a short cut across the corner of Brent's property. Max honed in on this mobile intrusion immediately and set off in rapid pursuit. In the fray that followed, the boy dismounted and ran hollering from the scene, but not before Max had torn at his clothes and left teeth marks on his leg. This was apparently the end of the road for Max, who was apprehended and incarcerated, pending a hearing. At the hearing he was ordered destroyed, whereupon Brent sought legal assistance and eventually caught up with me.

At the time I was contacted, Brent had already appealed the ruling, and a date for another hearing was set. Basically, Brent wondered if there was anything I could do to help him win back his dog. I was left in no doubt as to his attachment and dedication to his dog, and I knew that he would do anything to get Max back and prevent any further incidents. I didn't promise him anything, but I agreed to take a look at Max to evaluate his temperament and suggest any treatment that I thought might be appropriate. Mr. Thomas seized on this offer and within days had obtained a one-day furlough for Max in order for the evaluation to be carried out. It was a hot summer afternoon when Max and I first met outside the veterinary school. Brent was keen to show me his dog and put him through his paces. The dog was obviously his pride and joy. Temperamentally, Max appeared to be more stable than Sheena and showed fewer signs of anxiety. There were some subtle signs of submissiveness, however, and I felt that Max did not fall into the dominant category.

"May I?" I said, holding out my hand for the lead.

"Be my guest," responded Brent confidently.

I walked Max quickly, first in one direction, then the other, navigating tight turns and pausing occasionally to tell him to wait or to sit. He responded like a dream. Every command was obeyed immediately. He was like a well-trained soldier. I was able to crouch down on the ground, put one arm over Max's back, inspect his mouth, look in his eyes, hold his feet, and perform various other maneuvers that I wouldn't have been particularly keen to try out with Sheena. In the end, by virtue of Max's demeanor, workability, and tolerance, I was forced to the conclusion that he was a very well adjusted dog. I also viewed a videotape of Max with family members, who could do anything with him. On the good side, Max was friendly and reasonably confident. On the bad side, he would bark at and attempt to intimidate strangers approaching the house, and when chained up in the front yard would pull on the chain to try to get at uniformed visitors. He would also become agitated and aggressive when joggers or cyclists passed by the yard and would bark at and attempt to intimidate people approaching the car. Toll booth collectors were also subject to his unwanted attentions, and he would chase squirrels like there was no tomorrow. Basically, he was a guard dog who was a little too good at his job. Brent shamefully acknowledged that in earlier days he had encouraged Max's aggressive response to promote the guard dog side of his personality. I diagnosed territorial and predatory aggression and explained the toll booth collector syndrome to Brent. He wanted to know whether I would be prepared to repeat what I had said in a court of law and whether I could suggest any treatments. I told him that, for what it was worth, I would be very happy to explain to the court why Max was like he was and that I could make some utterances about diet and exercise and desensitization, but that I would find it necessary to stress the prevention aspects because of Max's great propensity for this type of behavior. He was happy to get any help he could, so he accepted my offer and we agreed to meet at the district court a couple of weeks later.

The big day arrived. Brent was extremely tense, knowing that Max's life was on the line. The proceedings started off with questioning of the dog-control officer, who droned on about his understanding of dogs such as Max. The judge, with his head resting on one hand, looked thoroughly disinterested and he doodled nonchalantly on his writing pad, pausing occasionally to roll his eyes heavenward and let out a deep sigh. Despite his apparent lack of interest, the judge nonetheless absorbed all the details of this, his ten thousandth civil suit (or thereabouts), as evidenced by his occasional timely interruption with pertinent comments. I was summoned after the dog-control officer and was able to paint a fairly accurate picture of Max's personality and likely response to treatment. What seemed to concern the judge the most was whether or not Max was a "vicious" dog. I really didn't think so and shared this opinion with the assembled throng. According to the dictionary definition, *vicious* literally means "addicted to vice, immoral, malignant, and depraved." There was no way I could ascribe any of these characteristics to Max, who was merely taking care of business as he saw fit. Admittedly, the behavior was not acceptable, but an explanation of what was driving it, and some brief words about prevention and treatment strategies, seemed to appease the judge, who gave Max the benefit of the doubt. With Max's freedom came certain conditions. Brent had to agree to work on retraining Max and to firmly secure Max to prevent any future escapes. Brent was very pleased and set off immediately to pick up Max. If every dog has its day, then this was Max's.

Treatment for Max included a switch to a low-protein diet, increasing his exercise to thirty minutes of aerobic exercise per day (within an enclosed area, of course), and counterconditioning and systematic desensitization (same as for Sheena). Brent was advised to make absolutely sure that Max was not able to escape again. I have spoken to him since and understand that all is well. There have been no further incidents, and in general Max seems to be a lot more composed, thanks to his new management system. Brent knows that he had a very close call and is suitably motivated to do everything he needs to do to keep Max in line. I feel confident that there will not be any further problems and am delighted that, with the judge's help, I was able to save Max's life.

On a final note, a few weeks after I saw Max, I got a call from a newspaper reporter writing for *The Patriot Ledger*. She introduced herself cheerfully and announced that she had heard about my involvement in the now famous Thomas case. We talked for some minutes; I repeated things when asked and paused occasionally in order that she could get the whole story down. As the interview began to draw to a close, however, I began to pick up a certain ironical tone in her voice, and I began to fear the worst—that I was talking to the opposition! This turned out to be the case, as I found out when I read the newspaper article later. "Pet behavior consultant Dr. Nicholas Dodman said that Max should be retrained by working with him to desensitize his fear of children. He suggested working Max with children to encourage a more favorable interaction. Whose children is he going to use? Yours? One thing is for sure, he's certainly not going to use mine." Ouch! I thought. The reporter obviously wasn't aware of how we manage desensitization programs and had taken the offensive. She didn't know, for example, that we insist that the dog be strictly under control and on leash, possibly using a halter or even a muzzle to prevent injury. In addition, the systematic nature of the desensitization itself—with the child first being presented to the dog at a distance, only being brought closer later in the program if the preceding steps are accomplished successfully—was clearly not familiar to her. Oh well, I thought, I guess all's fair in love and war—and this was indeed a sort of war, according to what I heard was going on in the community.

I continue to work with territorially aggressive dogs, although now the toll booth collector syndrome is only part of the picture. In the broadest definition of the syndrome, all sorts of people and all sorts of breeds are involved. Fear and anxiety are not the sole motivations for this behavior. Dominant dogs also display territoriality, barking at and intimidating visitors to the house, but there the similarity ends. Once a dominant dog has barked at you, jumped up on you, and slobbered on you, you're normally reasonably safe (as long as you watch out for those "blue suede shoes"). In other dogs, territorial aggression seems to stem from a combination of dominance and fear, and these dogs, in my experience, are the worst of all and the most difficult to treat. As always, the success of treatment depends not only on the age of the dog and the degree of the problem, but also on the commitment of the owners to stay with the program. The prognosis is good for young dogs with a problem of mild to moderate intensity if the owner can be relied upon to follow through. I have had some remarkable successes and believe that most owners can make significant improvements in their dog's behavior.

I am never quite sure which of the suggestions I make regarding treatment is going to be most effective for an individual. In some cases, owners feel in retrospect that increasing the animal's exercise was particularly effective; in others, dietary changes seem to have a profound effect; in yet others, control and training are central to the success of treatment. In most cases, however, it is the combination of elements that produces the best result. In refractory cases, it may be necessary to resort to medication. I frequently prescribe drugs such as propranolol to reduce anxiety and aggression without the side effects of sedation and inactivity. Doctors prescribe this medication for people with heart conditions to reduce anxiety and prevent sudden increases in heart rate and blood pressure. It is also used to control stage fright, fear of public speaking, and performance anxiety. More recently, it has found some application in the treatment of aggression in people. Propranolol is thought to exert its effect primarily by relaxing muscles. It does not adversely affect memory or learning, does not make patients sleepy, has few side effects, and is not addictive. What's more, it's extremely inexpensive. This and other benign medications can be used to facilitate the retraining of dogs that show fear-based territoriality.

Whatever line of treatment is engaged, it is important for owners to understand that improvement takes time. Retraining is something of an incremental process, with a relatively large initial improvement followed by continuing smaller gains. It is also important to continue to work with the dog to maintain the improvement. Even the best-trained Border Collie will revert if training is not ongoing, and territorial dogs that have gone through retraining are no exception. The bottom line is that something can be done to retrain dogs that are territorially aggressive and, for the most part, the treatment programs are quite successful. The biggest problem may be that folks are just not aware of these programs. Attention all mail carriers! Deliverance is at hand. Just write a note to the owners of problem dogs on your route and tell them to go visit a behaviorist. On second thought, maybe you should phone.

• TREATMENT FOR •

Territorial Aggression (Anxiety-Related or Fear-Related)

Territorial aggression manifests itself as aggression to strangers on the dog's own turf (home, surrounding streets, and car). People in uniforms are a particular target.

Treatment

1. Exercise is generally beneficial. A dog should have a minimum of twenty to thirty minutes of aerobic exercise *daily.*

2. There is some evidence that fearful dogs may benefit from low-protein diets (16 to 20 percent protein for dry rations). Low-protein diets should not be fed to growing dogs, pregnant bitches, and dogs with certain medical conditions.

3. Sharpen up on obedience training.

4. Desensitization with counterconditioning (for fear-based cases). Desensitization involves acclimating the dog to a person it is afraid of by gradual exposure, allowing the dog to become comfortable at progressively increasing levels of challenge. This is often done in association with counterconditioning (e.g., food reward).

5. Limit the dog's urination to one spot in the yard.

6. If prescribed, give the dog medication, e.g., propranolol (Inderal).

7. Use a shake can when the dog fails to respond to a verbal command in the car.

CHAPTER 4

A Bone to Pick

W hen two dogs that are both well versed in matters pertaining to canine etiquette meet for the first time or after a period of absence, they seek to establish rank by means of body language. Assuming some level of dominance in each dog, they will, at least for a short while, look directly at each other. Depending on what each dog sees, it will either hold its gaze, symbolizing superiority, or avert its eyes, signaling deference (or subordinance). Most of these visual exchanges, accompanied by subtle changes in posture, occur so quickly that the dog owner is hardly aware of them. Extremely dominant dogs seem to call out every other dog they meet, while most others, on viewing such a dog, wisely decline the contest. Fearful dogs may even preempt the dominance rituals, meeting challengers with eyes already averted and tail tucked. When you think about it, people behave in much the same way. Successful leaders often appear to go out of their way to meet people and approach them with erect posture and a steady gaze. These leaders often invade other people's personal space, standing uncomfortably close and almost literally breathing down others' necks. Firm handshakes, arm squeezing, and one-arm hugs are also high on the human dominance body-language scale. If people try out these power handshakes on me, I sometimes hang on to their hand for several long seconds. This usually reverses the momentum. (My wife, who is also a veterinarian, tells me it's because I am like a dominant dog.)

If the stare alone doesn't do the trick for a dominant dog, the animal is forced to escalate its challenge. At this point, owners who are not in complete control may find that their dog is walking steadily toward the other dog, muscles tense, tail raised, and ears pricked. If this escalation doesn't have the desired effect, there is a progression into frank aggression, perhaps starting with an extremely ominous low growl and lip lift, progressing quickly to the fight-and-bite mode. Arbitration is not on the dog's agenda. Extremely dominant dogs will usually become involved in occasional dog fights. Owners are often perplexed that a dog like this may be aggressive to one out of ten dogs, while after a brief encounter with others, it may start to play. All these observations are explicable on the basis of dominance and subordinance. Dominant dogs will fight only if their authority is challenged or if valued resources are threatened. Some owners appear to be viewed as valued resources and are possessively guarded by their dogs against encroachments by other dogs or people.

Dominance struggles between dogs are not confined to new encounters and are not always easily settled. When a dominance issue is unresolved between two dogs, a feud will continue until one dog is clearly established as the victor and the other as the vanquished. This kind of problem between dogs within the home, propagated by interference by the owner, is referred to as sibling rivalry (although the dogs don't necessarily have to be related in any way). One memorable ongoing case of sibling rivalry that I became involved in was in the home of a lawyer client of mine. The woman, Bertha Weiss, lived with two large Chesapeake Bay Retrievers and a pack of American Rat Terriers. Her elegant home was dog heaven, and no expense was spared for her surrogate family. The dogs had the run of the house, elegant outdoor kennels, and the best food and veterinary treatment; some of the little ones slept on silk pillows. They even had their own personal portrait photographer. I had first seen Bertha because of an aggression problem she had with one of her Chessies. Chesapeake Bay Retrievers were originally bred to protect fishing boats in Chesapeake Bay, so it is not entirely surprising to come across the occasional zealot. It turned out that Bertha was more interested in gaining control of the dog than in preventing the aggression, as she lived on her own and the dogs were her security system. We had a few training sessions together and made some progress, but that was not to be the last of my involvement with Bertha's pack.

The sibling rivalry problem came to light later, almost as an incidental problem, and involved infighting in her terrier pack. These little dogs were perfectly fine while Bertha was away, but the minute she walked in the door at night, battle would commence. Although the middle-rankers, who were called Matt, Pete, and Jake, got on reasonably well, the upper echelon, Sarah and Blossom, would ferociously attack the most submissive dogs, Lisa and Kim, sometimes inflicting bite wounds that needed veterinary treatment. At this time my wife was acting as Bertha's veterinarian, so we got involved in trying to help her with the problem. Bertha was told in no uncertain terms that she was facilitating the problem by constantly reinforcing the status of the underdogs. Most people feel a need to support the underdog, so Bertha's response was understandable; nevertheless, it was one that doesn't cut any ice with those of the pack mentality. What she was doing by her constant interventions was actually perpetuating the vendetta. She would do things such as push Sarah and Blossom out of the way so that Lisa and Kim could feed. She would rescue them from any trouble and protect them on her lap, petting and comforting them in times of woe. This was exactly the wrong way to respond in front of the dominant ones, and the problem was rapidly getting much worse. Bertha just couldn't help herself. As sensitive and intelligent as she was, she just couldn't bring herself to be "unkind" to her underdogs.

"Yes, yes, I know. I should be a little tougher," she would chuckle, "but they're such poor babies, I just have to help them."

Despite continued warnings, Bertha persisted until one day Kim was bitten badly. I didn't witness the results of this attack by Blossom, but the damage was severe enough for Bertha to have Kim put to sleep. She could easily have afforded the veterinary care, but I believe she saw euthanasia as the most humane solution to the problem. As you may have guessed, however, the problem didn't stop there. Lisa now became the lone pariah dog and, predictably, was comforted and protected by Bertha. The problem had become so serious that even a reversal of strategy by Bertha would not have prevented the events that ensued. The struggle between the dogs had become so intense that Lisa was at constant risk of being dealt grievous bodily harm by any of the others. At this point, the only real solution would have been to find another home for Lisa and somehow persuade Bertha to rethink her interactions with the remaining dogs, but before my wife and I had an opportunity to readvise, we received an emergency call from Bertha.

"You have to come quickly—something terrible has happened. Lisa has been attacked, and she's bleeding all over the place. I have to go to work—I have an extremely important meeting that I must attend. Will you please come to the house and pick Lisa up and give me a call later to let me know how she is?"

Luckily for Bertha, we were able to respond immediately. We jumped into my Jeep and drove to Bertha's house at slightly above the speed limit. The house key was under the mat, and we let ourselves in. It was almost like being the first to arrive on a murder scene. Everything was quiet except for the ticking of Bertha's many clocks. We made our way across a sea of Persian rugs to the stairway leading to the scene of the crime, the upstairs bedroom. As we walked into the bedroom we could see a trail of blood leading across the white rug and over the silk sheets of the massive bed Bertha shared with her dogs. Finally a badly bitten Lisa came into view, quaking in the corner. The poor dog looked up pathetically. Her white coat was bloodstained, and there were puncture wounds in one hind leg. The whole limb was swollen and bruised from a crushing bite, and two skin flaps hung loosely from the lacerated area. After inspecting her wounds carefully and checking her vital signs, we cleaned her up and put her into a padded crate for transportation back to our house. The other terriers, which Bertha had confined to a backyard enclosure, looked a little sheepish as we left. The Chessies barked, of course, and had the gratification of believing that they had driven us away.

When we got back home, we sutured up Lisa as best we could and then called Bertha. She started talking about euthanasia again.

We tried to dissuade her from this extreme solution to her problem and suggested that placing Lisa in a new home would be a more reasonable approach. After all, there was nothing wrong with Lisa other than the situation she found herself in. Bertha decided to think about this for a while; she was concerned that a new home would be too distressing for Lisa. Lisa was returned to Bertha's house twenty-four hours after the assault, and we held our breath while Bertha weighed her options. We had done everything we could do, and now it was up to Bertha—after all, it is owners who ultimately make the decisions. Sadly, Bertha spent a little too long deliberating, and there was a second attack in which Lisa's abdomen was lacerated exposing part of her gut. This time Bertha couldn't get hold of us, so she called the emergency service at the veterinary school. The staff there elegantly repaired the physical damage to Lisa, but this time Bertha knew that she had to make a decision quickly to prevent further incidents. She decided to have Sarah *and* Blossom put to sleep.

Bertha's tragedy highlights the importance of understanding your pack and the fateful consequences of the wrong approach to management. Most cases of sibling rivalry respond well to treatment if corrective measures are taken early enough. Treatment of sibling rivalry involves reinforcing the position of the more dominant dog and ignoring the more subordinate one. This goes against the grain for us humans, but it is the only way to turn around sibling rivalry problems. The dominant dog should be fed first, petted first, played with first, and so on. Basically, the dominant dog should be treated with priority in all matters. In the event of a tussle breaking out between the dogs, they should be distracted with a command or loud noise. It is unwise to break up fights by dragging dogs apart by the scruff of the neck, as this can result in aggression being redirected toward you. Queen Elizabeth II fell into this trap not too long ago when she tried to break up a fight between her Corgis. A behaviorist later remarked that it would have been better if she had dropped one of her solid silver trays on the stone floor to break up the fight. (Maybe she will next time.) After a fight has been successfully broken up, you should acknowledge the dominant dog's status by praising and petting it. The subordinate dog should not be catered to (unless, of course, it has been injured). If there is any reason to think that two dogs might hurt each other, both should be muzzled, and then they can be left to fight it out—it is quite possible for a dominance dispute to be settled without actual biting. Eventually, with the owners' continued support of the dominant dog's position, the problem should subside. One other important aspect of the treatment of sibling rivalry is that owners should establish their dominance over both (or all) of their dogs by working on an obedience program. There should be only one overall boss . . . you. When the owner calls time, no dog should bark.

Dominance is probably the most common cause of intraspecies aggression in dogs, and males are most frequently involved. This is the only type of aggressive behavior that has been shown to respond dramatically to neutering, which should be the first line of treatment for an intact male. You might think that neutering works because it makes the dog less dominant, but this is not so. As it turns out, when a male is neutered, it no longer smells like a male to other male dogs. In fact, other dogs may possibly mistake the emasculated male for a female. All a neutered dog notices is that everyone else suddenly starts being a lot nicer to him. The result is fewer fights. I wish such a simple and effective treatment option were available for other types of dog-on-dog aggression, or for dominant bitches. Curiously, dominant bitches seem more aggressive following spaying, perhaps because neutered females no longer have a source of progesterone in their body. It's a great pity that bitches can't have their jets cooled by spaying, because bitches fighting bitches accounts for some of the more ferocious battles we see—witness Bertha's problems.

Medical treatment can also be a helpful adjunct to behavioral approaches in severe or refractory cases of sibling rivalry. Since dominance is involved, it is no surprise to find out that Prozac and look-alikes can be used effectively (see chapter 1). Logically, the dog to treat is the dominant one. The use of Prozac in this situation will likely reinforce the dog's dominance, which paradoxically reduces aggression. Elevated brain levels of serotonin resulting from Prozac treatment seem to stabilize the dog's mood and increase its overall confidence. It is as if the dog no longer has so much to prove. Synthetic progesterones have also been used to treat dominance-related fighting, but their serious side effects, such as diabetes, make them a last resort.

Not all dog fighting is due to dominance. Fear may also be a factor, and in some cases there may even be a predatory motivation. One fear-related case that I dealt with recently came to me via our PetFax consulting service (which is a national fax, e-mail, or regular-mail behavioral consulting service operated out of Tufts). The subject was a two-year-old female Labrador called Susie, who attacked every dog she saw. This is not a normal dominance pattern, so I knew something else was going on. I found out that Susie had been viciously attacked by another dog when she was young. She was three months old at the time and had been out in the front yard when a neighboring dog vaulted the fence and savagely assaulted her for no known reason (predatory factors may have been involved). This attack occurred in the critical period of Susie's life when learning occurs readily. During this period, isolated events often leave an indelible impression. This appeared to be what had happened with Susie, because from that day forth, she regarded every other dog as a potential enemy. While she was still young, she would cower and back away from other dogs, but in time she learned to come forward and deal with the problem herself. Susie acquired a modicum of dominance as she matured, making this proactive approach possible. The combination of overwhelming fear and dominance made Susie a constant threat to caninekind. The essential component of the treatment program I suggested was a customized desensitization program designed to restore Susie's confidence in other dogs. A program such as this takes time and patience, but Susie's owners were up to it, and at last report were making steady progress. As mentioned earlier, fears such as this never really go away completely, but they can be usefully modified by desensitization, which makes life much more pleasant for both dog and owner.

Another case of dog-on-dog aggression that I saw at our animal hospital was a composite of fear-related aggression and predatory aggression. This dog, Bear, a one-year-old spayed female Old English Sheepdog, had been bought from a pet store when she was three months old. The primary complaint of her owner, Diana Harrison, was aggression to other dogs, especially to puppies and other bitches. Diana, a Ph.D. student at Boston University, liked to take Bear for walks on Boston Common, and she particularly enjoyed letting her run off-leash. Although Diana would try to time her visits to the Common to avoid meeting other dogs, she was rarely successful in this endeavor, as most times another dog walker or one of the city's many strays would show up. Bear's response to other dogs was completely unpredictable. Sometimes she would run and attack the other dog with little or no provocation, and other times she would stand her ground with a blank look on her face as the other dog came over, attacking at the last minute after what appeared to be a friendly approach.

Bear's whole conception of what other dogs were about was a bit off, and it seemed that she was totally lacking in knowledge of the signals of dominance and subordinance. I have seen this apparent absence of any understanding of canine etiquette previously, in dogs that were orphaned and hand-reared and in dogs that, for various reasons, were prematurely separated from their littermates. It appears that the rough and tumble of puppyhood early in the socialization period (from three to twelve weeks) is necessary for dogs to learn how to signal their rank and how to acknowledge properly victory or defeat. Orphans often exhibit inappropriate canine responses during encounters with other dogs, seemingly lacking the necessary communication skills. Bear was certainly confused, and I could only guess that she had some kind of dysfunctional history prior to Diana's acquiring her. I know that puppy-mill dogs are weaned early, as younger puppies are a more salable commodity; maybe this had something to do with it.

Not only were Bear's dog manners inappropriate, but she was also underconfident, as shown by her apparent fear of other bitches. Prior to a scrape, she would often show signs of nervousness, first approaching and then withdrawing from the other dog. If she actually attacked, it would be in the form of a snap-and-run attack, sometimes snapping or biting two or three times in quick succession. On one occasion Diana had been walking Bear down by the Charles River when a white terrier of unknown breed showed up. Bear was, as usual, off-lead, and the white terrier, a bitch, approached Bear with head held low, tail tucked and wagging. Bear immediately turned into the proverbial land shark and snapped repeatedly at the terrier, which whimpered, yelped, and then ran for her life. Diana reported that on another occasion a few weeks earlier, Bear had been approached by a rather large and dominant-looking retriever bitch. The other dog proceeded toward Bear, growling and frothing at the mouth. Bear stood motionless and was attacked. Diana tried to break up the ensuing fight and got bitten herself—by Bear, she thought. Her hand was still bandaged at the time of our interview.

My assessment of Bear in light of these stories was that she was a confused and fearful dog. As if that weren't enough, she also attacked very small dogs and puppies, and in these instances seemed to know exactly what she was doing. The circumstances of these attacks on small dogs and puppies always involved Bear's chasing and biting the running victim without displaying any apparent emotion except perhaps a little excitement. She would run toward the fleeing creature, picking up speed, and finally, as she drew alongside, she would nip at it until it got away, or until an owner intervened. This sounded a lot like predatory behavior to me. Sheep-herding breeds seem particularly prone to this, as predatory behavior is a fundamental component of their repertoire. The genetic inclination of a particular breed is frequently an important factor in behavior problems and must not be overlooked. I once had a case in which a retriever with separation anxiety herded shoes at the rate of one every fifteen minutes during his owner's absence. She could tell how long she'd been away by counting the number of shoes in the pile on her return. Likewise, it is not surprising when a Rottweiler displays protective behavior or when a Chesapeake Bay Retriever or Dalmatian guards overenthusiastically.

Whether genetics was a factor or not, Bear had a problem (or two), and I had to deal with it. Unfortunately, most of the things that I suggested to Diana were not acceptable to her, or were impossible for her to do. She couldn't, or didn't want to, change the place where she walked Bear, so avoidance was not an option. She pretty much refused to keep Bear on a leash, as she felt that it was an infringement on Bear's civil liberties that would deprive both Bear and her of a favorite daily ritual. In addition, Diana would not hear of having Bear wear any type of muzzle. I could see that it wasn't going to be easy. On the good side, Diana was an extremely pleasant person to work with and was willing to try almost anything else that was suggested. We discussed the use of a dog halter for training sessions in which Bear's obedience and tolerance to other dogs would be gradually shaped. Diana seemed happy enough to work in this way but chose, in the first instance at least, to use a choke collar rather than the halter. Once under control, Bear was to be introduced to other dogs in a gradual way, along the lines of a desensitization program. Although I didn't think it was a major factor in this case, I asked Diana to trim Bear's bangs. This is often a good move with an Old English Sheepdog, which can, particularly if nervous, be suddenly surprised by approaching people or dogs. Diana agreed to do this. Finally, because of the overwhelmingly self-reinforcing properties of predatory behavior, aversive therapy was deemed to be the only solution to Bear's problems in this area, and Diana was asked to carry an air horn with her on walks so that she could rudely interrupt Bear's chasing episodes.

Diana acted on these suggestions for a few weeks and was having some limited success, but I felt that things were not progressing as rapidly as they should, so I had her return to the hospital for a hands-on troubleshooting session with a friend of mine who is a dog trainer. I arranged for a few dogs to be paraded in front of Bear (who was on lead) to see how Diana was coping. It became apparent before too long that she still had a long way to go. She was far too tense and was transmitting her fears and concerns to Bear instead of instilling confidence. The trainer showed Diana how to control Bear more effectively so that she could proceed with the desensitization program. By the end of the session, she was doing much better, and left reinvigorated and ready to try again. I attempted once more to talk her into using the halter, which I felt would have facilitated her leadership role, but she still preferred to use a choke chain, believing that the halter was a kind of muzzle that would impair Bear's ability to defend herself. Nothing could be further from the truth, but I couldn't persuade her of that. Because of her insistence on using a choke chain, I made sure that she had follow-up sessions with the trainer. Using a choke chain properly takes years of practice. Undercorrection with a choke chain is ineffective, and overcorrection is inhumane. In addition, timing is absolutely critical. In any case, it is not appropriate for every dog or dog owner.

Several weeks and many training sessions later, Diana was extremely pleased with the progress she had made. She had a much better understanding of how her behavior could affect Bear's interpretation of events and was a lot slicker when it came to control. I think the main thing that she had learned was confidence in dealing with Bear, and Bear responded accordingly. Desensitization was progressing smoothly, and Boston Common had become a safer place for other dogs. However, Diana knew she would have to keep at it if this new-found progress was to be maintained.

Dogs can be aggressive to other dogs for a number of different reasons, including dominance, fear, and predation; each has been looked at in this chapter. I have devised a scoring system whereby these individual traits can be quantified. I may, for example, give a dog a score of nine out of ten in the dominance department, one out of ten in the fear department, and two out of ten in the predatory department. This kind of dog would be expected to pick occasional fights with other dogs. Dogs with high fear scores may have been scared by another dog and may react as Susie did, while dogs with intense predatory instincts are more prone to attack smaller, rapidly moving dogs. I find this canine equivalent of the Meyers-Briggs personality profile quite useful for predicting certain types of behavior, including dog-on-dog aggression, and for determining the motivation behind other aggressive incidents. Restoring the correct social balance is essential in the treatment of dominance-related problems (neutering of males may be useful toward this end). For fearful dogs, desensitization is always the cornerstone of treatment, and quite respectable results should be expected. Predatory aggression is the really difficult one to control, but sometimes simply explaining the cause of the problem to the owner can provide them with the information they need to prevent unwanted assaults.

• TREATMENT FOR •

Dog-on-Dog Aggression Related to Dominance

The dog is aggressive to some other dogs and displays both dominant posturing (body held erect, tenseness, tail held up, eyes fixed
on other dog) in the presence of other dogs and other signs of dominance at home (being overly confident or pushy).

Treatment

1. Gain control over the dog through obedience work and the dominance program described in chapter 1.
2. Physically restrain the dog when necessary, using a halter, for
   example.
3. Neuter males.
4. Employ pharmacotherapy in extreme cases.
5. In sibling rivalry situations, support the more dominant dog.

Dog-on-Dog Aggression Related to Fear

This involves more-generalized aggression to all dogs or dogs of a
certain size or breed. The dog's history may be important (for example, aversive events may have occurred in the dog's life). Posturing
may be a clue, as for example if the dog backs off with its tail
tucked.

Treatment

1. Desensitization with counterconditioning usually works well.
2. Pharmacotherapy (with, for example, propranolol, buspirone, or
   Prozac-like medication) may be needed in difficult cases.

Dog-on-Dog Aggression Related to Predatory Drive

This kind of aggression is often directed at small dogs that are moving quickly. Dogs with this problem also have well-developed predatory behavior in regard to other small animals (such as squirrels and
cats).

Treatment

1. Avoid animals that may seem like targets.
2. Aversive therapy may be effective.

CHAPTER 5

Two Dogs and a Baby

One afternoon I received a call from a young woman who said in a trembling voice, "My name is Robin White. My local vet gave me your name. He said you might be able to help me. The problem is that my dog is trying to go after my new baby, and to tell you the truth, I'm very scared."

"Tell me exactly what's going on," I said.

"We have a couple of field-strain English Springer Spaniels," she said. "They are wonderful dogs and have never been aggressive to anybody. The only thing they do that could even remotely be construed as aggressive is to try to catch wild animals, like rabbits and squirrels. They will also chase birds and cats. When I came back from the hospital with the baby a few days ago, I sat on the couch cradling the baby, and my husband brought in the two dogs. Samson, the male, was wriggling with excitement, and he ran across to see me, but when he reached me he stopped dead and sniffed at the baby's blanket. It was as though he wanted to explore the strange object I was holding in my arms. Then he began whimpering and whining and got into a frenzy. He started to mouth and pull at the blanket. There was no controlling him. My husband just had to take him outside. The only time I've ever seen Samson like this before was at a friend's house. They had cats, and he reacted the same way toward them."

"How has Samson been with the baby since the incident? Is he getting any better, or is he getting worse?" I asked.

"He's definitely not getting better. It's hopeless. I tried putting him down in the cellar, but he barked so loudly that the neighbors across the street complained. And he damaged the cellar door trying to get out. I even tried putting him outside, but he damaged the vinyl siding on the house by biting and scratching it, trying to get back in. Eventually he tore through a screen and did get in. Nothing helps. What on earth can I do?"

Having listened to Robin's story, I was quite alarmed. I realized she needed help urgently.

"I want you to keep the dogs and the baby completely separate tonight, and I would like you to come see me tomorrow morning, first thing," I advised her. "We need to talk. Can your husband come along, too?" She said he could, and the appointment was set.

The next morning, Robin and her husband, Barry, showed up right on time. Their dogs were the best-looking pair of Springers I have ever seen. Robin seemed pleased to see me, but Barry looked a little grim. I wasn't sure whether it was the going-to-see-the-behaviorist syndrome or whether he was nervous about what might transpire. I first assessed the dogs by observing their interaction with people in the waiting room. Their manners were impeccable, and they were respectably obedient. They had obviously been well trained at some point but were a little rusty, judging from their sluggish response to commands. After working with the dogs for a few minutes, I sat down with Robin and Barry in the consulting room, and the formal session began. I asked them all kinds of questions about the dogs, including where they had obtained them, what their sires and dams were like, what the dogs ate, and how they spent their days. Other than the earlier report of extremely well developed predatory instincts, there was nothing remarkable to note. The Whites shed more light upon the predatory aspects of Samson's behavior by telling me a story about what had happened when the family visited a man with a pet parakeet. They had warned the man about Samson's bird-chasing tendencies, but the man scoffed, saying that his bird was too smart to get caught. He proceeded to open the cage, whereupon Samson darted toward the fluttering bird and engulfed it in the blink of an eye. Barry raced forward and pried open the dog's jaws to release the dazed parakeet, which, fortunately, survived to flutter again. If I needed any further evidence of Samson's exceptional predatory drive, this was it. The diagnostic net was narrowing. Neither of the dogs showed any dominance-related aggression to the Whites, and neither was noticeably fearful. Apparently the bitch, Delilah, became mildly excited by Samson's reaction to the baby, but she was not the instigator. I diagnosed predatory behavior as the underlying cause of Samson's peculiar reaction to the baby, with Delilah packing along for the ride.

"Would you like to see for yourself?" Robin asked. "My mother is looking after the baby outside. I can go and get them if you like."

"Okay," I said a little hesitantly, "but I want to have both dogs on leashes, and Barry, if there is any problem, I would like you to take charge of the dogs and remove them from the room." We all agreed on the plan.

The baby was brought into the room. Neither dog paid much attention. Robin sat down with the baby on her lap and called the male Springer to her. He walked over to her slowly and casually, sniffed the bundle on her lap, and then walked off.

"He's not doing it now," exclaimed Robin. "Would you believe it?"

We tried on several other occasions to generate the reported response, but there was nothing doing. I pushed back my chair.

"They've got other things to think about in this hospital environment," I ventured. "I think it would be better if I came and saw them at home. You live close by, so if you don't mind, I'll swing by tonight on my way home and take a look. I may have to change my diagnosis when I see them in action, but I doubt that will be the case. It is highly significant that Samson's response to your friend's cats was the same as it is to the baby. If predatory instincts are involved, you will have to be very careful. I don't want to alarm you, but some people believe that predatory dogs may mistakenly perceive a struggling, crying infant as wounded prey . . . and you know what predators do to prey. The potential consequences are so serious that we can't afford to take any chances."

"I don't want to get rid of him, Doctor," said Barry tensely. "That's not an option for us." I didn't argue, but I thought that he would change his mind if I was unsuccessful in turning this situation around.

"I'll work with you to try to prevent that, Barry, but for the time being, and probably for a good while into the future, you must never let the dog and the baby be alone together. I want you to promise me that when the baby and the dog are together, there will be two of you around—one in charge of the baby and the other in charge of the dogs. By in charge of the dogs, I mean that Samson and Delilah should be on lead and under control." Barry nodded. I saw his shoulders visibly slump with relief that I hadn't immediately told him it would be necessary to get rid of the dogs. Now there was a chance for them. No matter how slim, he wanted to take it. However, I kept having terrible flashbacks to a story I had heard about a couple whose dog pushed through a supposedly closed door while they were sleeping, took the baby from the crib, and ate it. They only found out the next day, when the dog was X-rayed. A shiver ran down my spine, but I forced a half smile in Robin's direction.

"Here is what you have to do to help Samson," I said. "I would like him to get at least thirty minutes of aerobic exercise every day, and I want you to change his diet to a nonperformance ration. I also want you to work hard on obedience training with him so that he will obey you instantly, even under difficult circumstances. If he calms down and you have control, we will work on a program of gradual introductions between him and the baby, rewarding him for remaining calm and directing him if he begins to lose control and starts whimpering. Above all, barring training sessions, keep the dogs and the baby apart."

"The exercise part should be easy," said Barry. "I'm a runner and I go out almost every day. I can just bring him with me."

"That will be fine," I acknowledged. "There is one other option that I should probably mention. It may be beneficial to put him on some kind of medication, but this would be secondary to the treatment I have described. If I confirm the predatory nature of his response when I see him, we can try putting him on either the antidepressant amitriptyline or an anxiety-reducing drug called buspirone. Both medications have been shown in the laboratory to have powerful antipredatory effects."

They appeared to understand all that had been said, and we shook hands and parted. I watched them leave through the front door of the hospital, babe in arms and dogs in tow, and couldn't help but reflect on the gravity of their situation.

Later that afternoon, I set off for the Whites' house, arriving there a little after five o'clock. Robin came out, accompanied by Samson and Delilah, who were obviously thrilled to have a visitor. We watched the dogs romp for a while and engaged in a little light conversation before entering the Whites' immaculately kept ranch house to deal with the business at hand. Robin's mother and a friend were on either side of the door, standing guard like sentinels, as we headed for the kitchen. The first maneuver we tried was not particularly enlightening. Robin sat down on the couch next to me and cradled the young baby while her mother ushered the dogs into the room. Samson came up and investigated a little, but mild curiosity was the only reaction that I saw. Robin suggested changing the baby's diaper because she thought the baby's crying would trigger the response. As predicted, the baby did cry a little during the diaper changing. Samson became slightly agitated at this, but the most interesting thing was that Delilah flew into the bedroom where the crib was, put her paws up on the side of the crib, and began weaving and jumping up and down as if searching for something—which, of course, was exactly what she was doing. When Robin put the baby into the crib, both dogs became really anxious and started to whine and wiggle, pushing themselves up against the crib with apparently single-minded intent. They were on a mission, driven from within. Samson's whining became even louder.

"What shall I do?" said Robin.

"Give the dogs a command," I replied. "Tell them to sit."

Robin tightened her hold on the two leashes and issued a firm command directed at both dogs. Amazingly, both dogs did sit, but Samson continued to whine.

"Do I praise him? He's whining, so if I praise him, it will just encourage that behavior, right?" said Robin. "What do I do?"

"Tell them to lie down," I said. Robin tried this without much luck.

"What do I do now?" she said.

"Just take the dogs, walk out of the bedroom into the living room, and get them under control out there."

"But if I leave the bedroom, I've got to come back in again, and the same thing is going to happen."

"Let's do it anyway," I suggested, realizing that Robin was stressed and would probably not be able to absorb much information under the circumstances. "We can regroup later and come up with a better plan of action."

Once we were in the living room and the dogs had been subdued, Robin and I resumed our conversation and decided on a game plan. First, one of the dogs was to be removed from the scene for a week or two, perhaps to stay with the in-laws. This would make it a lot easier for Robin, who just couldn't handle two dogs and attend to the baby at the same time. After some discussion we decided to farm out Samson, as Delilah was the easier of the two to control. Barry was not there during this session, but I explained to Robin that I wanted him to work hard on obedience-training both dogs so that they would be under better control. We went back over the retraining exercises, including the specifics of how to introduce Delilah to the baby. Sessions would be conducted only when Barry was at home so that he could manage Delilah while Robin looked after the baby. Delilah would be led toward the baby and required to sit and stay. She would be praised and petted almost continuously as a reward for remaining calm. If she began to show signs of anxiousness, she would be led away and brought back again a short while later, perhaps not being allowed quite so close to the baby the second time around. And so on.

Robin was happy with this plan and said she would relay it to Barry when he came home. She also agreed to medicate Samson with the drug buspirone in the hopes that this would reduce his predatory drive somewhat. Samson's absence would give the medication a chance to kick in before the next introductions between him and the baby.

The session over, I left the house just as Barry arrived, and I was able to spend a few moments with him explaining what had transpired and reiterating the message about training. I asked him to stay in touch and pointed out that this was not the end of our interaction, only the beginning.

A week later, Robin called back with good news. Fortunately, the buspirone appeared to be working well, as Samson seemed much calmer. As behavior-modification therapy was being used simultaneously, it was not possible to ascribe the improvement exclusively to the medication, but either way, I was delighted with the results and basically told them to continue with more of the same. Shortly after this follow-up conversation, Barry, encouraged by the early success, reintroduced Samson to the baby. Apparently Samson remained calm and composed, almost nonchalant, even when confronted by the dreaded diaper-changing ritual. Without consulting with me, the Whites allowed Samson back into their home, and life returned to normal. I found out about these happenings during my next telephone call and welcomed the good news, wondering about the apparently miraculous results of treatment.

There was one small twist at the end of the story, however. When the buspirone was discontinued after one month of successful treatment, Samson had a resurgence of his predatory behavior toward the baby. I immediately suggested full-scale safety measures and reinstitution of the medication. Once again, Samson's behavior improved, and he was maintained on this medication for another couple of months before being weaned off. This time there was no return of the unwanted behavior, and a long-term follow-up indicated that Samson had finally taken to the new baby, accepting her into the pack. The case was closed.

If the Whites had been better informed about what to expect when the new baby arrived, could they have done anything to prevent the problem? In their case, I doubt whether any measures would have been 100 percent effective, as the behavior the dogs were showing was innate. However, to be forewarned is to be forearmed. If they had made an appointment with me before the baby's arrival, they could have prepared themselves for what might be in store and arranged things a little differently. From the behaviorist's point of view, the most important thing to determine in such a prenatal appointment is the underlying temperament of the dog, because predatory dogs, dominant dogs, and fearful dogs all present different challenges. Dogs with different character traits may be problematic at different times and under different circumstances, and their management and treatment can be quite distinct.

Predatory aggression is thought to be at the heart of some of the most serious dog attacks directed toward babies, and should be ruled out first. There are approximately ten infant deaths per year in the United States that arise from misdirection of this innate canine behavior. Fortunately, the incidence of this condition is so low that one is probably more likely to get struck on the head by a falling brick than to have a catastrophe of this nature occur; but however rare the phenomenon, it does occur. As a dog's natural behavior with respect to newborn pups is that of a protector, infanticidal behavior may seem enigmatic, but there is a possible explanation. It could be that the dog doesn't immediately recognize the newborn child as a pack member, so the tragedy that results is really a case of mistaken identity. In support of this, the majority of human infants on the receiving end of attacks by predatory dogs are less than one week old.

Although dogs with different temperaments present different challenges to the new parent, there are some generic strategies that can be employed to minimize the impact of the new arrival and facilitate the introduction of the new pack member. In general, it is a good idea to make any changes in the environment or daily routine as far in advance as possible so that the baby doesn't get the blame for the upheaval. It may, for example, be helpful to prevent the dog from going into the baby's room at night several months before the baby actually arrives. If the dog will have to stay in another part of the house, then this change should also be effected as far in advance as possible. Another suggestion is to carry around a swaddled doll to represent the new arrival and to rehearse various baby maneuvers in the dog's presence, simultaneously rewarding the dog for calm behavior and obedience. Some even go so far as to suggest taking the dog for a walk with the doll in a stroller. This certainly attracts some strange looks from the neighbors, but helps the dog get accustomed to new procedures and routines. I believe that one of the most useful measures is to make a tape recording of the sounds of a baby crying and to desensitize the dog to the sounds. As with the Whites' dog, the sound of a baby crying seems to be one of the things that stirs up a dog the most. One widely touted piece of advice is to bring home from the hospital an article of the baby's clothing (not a diaper) to allow the dog to become acclimated to the baby's scent before the actual introduction. The Whites had actually tried this trick and it was obviously not successful for them. A diaper should not be used as the olfactory vehicle since dogs are programmed to eat the excrement of newborn pups and may choke on or develop bowel obstructions from a rapidly expanding cellulose diaper.

At the homecoming, it is important to introduce the dog and the baby in a gradual fashion. The husband should wait outside with the newborn baby while the new mother enters the home to greet the dog, which will not have seen her for several days. Once the excitement is over, the dog should be put on lead and instructed to sit or lie down while the baby is brought in. This whole sequence should be conducted in a calm and controlled manner, with dog and baby both carefully chaperoned. The dog may then be walked slowly, but not tenuously, toward the baby. At any sign of balking, the process should be aborted and the dog simply led off, to be reintroduced more gradually over the hours or days that follow. If the greeting goes well, the dog should be allowed to sniff the baby. In most instances, the dog will then proceed to treat the baby with indifference. As mentioned for predatory dogs, it is particularly important to be vigilant in the early weeks and to prevent the dog and baby from being together unattended *at any time*.

Whether a dog is dominant or fearful, if the owner's attention is directed almost exclusively to a new baby, the dog will become aware of this shift of attention and will react in some way. Dominant dogs may become more possessive of their owners, while fearful dogs may develop anxiety-related problems. Perceiving a problem, owners often try to make it up to the dog by paying it a lot more attention when the baby is asleep, but the dog soon figures out what is going on, and guess who gets the blame. Not the owner, that's for sure. If not actively prevented, a sibling rivalry situation can arise between dog and baby. For prevention or cure of this thorny problem, it is best to share your attention with the dog when the baby is around while paying it little attention at other times. Such a strategy will minimize the psychological impact of the new arrival and will help to endear the baby to the dog, which is now forced to the opposite opinion—that good things happen only when the baby is around. To achieve the end result takes considerable juggling on the part of busy parents, who have to care for the baby and indulge the dog simultaneously, but the bottom line is that it is well worth the trouble. In this way, the potential problems of sibling rivalry or anxiety-based conditions can be prevented or treated.

Had Samson and Delilah been dominant, they would have presented a different problem for the Whites, because dominant dogs are rarely a problem around very young children. The dominant dog can be recognized by its outgoing character, willfulness, and possessiveness. When the baby is first brought home, the dominant dog may sniff around and show some mild interest, but later it will probably ignore the baby and act as if the infant doesn't even exist. Problems between dominant dogs and children more often occur when the child is around one and a half or two years old and is beginning to toddle confidently and become more invasive. This is the time when parents know they must put safety covers on electrical outlets, protect stairways with kiddy gates, put their crystal out of the child's reach, and keep the knife drawer closed. Dominant dogs can be just one more environmental hazard for children of this age, and steps must be taken to avoid accidents. These dogs do not take kindly to being explored by curious, newly mobile youngsters, and after trying to move away a couple of times or issuing a low growl, they may signify their extreme displeasure by means of a snap or bite. Unfortunately, these bites are usually directed toward the child's face, and noses have been lost in this way. Accidents of this nature are tragic because they are entirely avoidable if owners understand how the dog perceives the child's advances and take steps to prevent such encounters.

Dominance situations arising directly between dogs and children should be addressed before they occur by applying a "prevention is better than cure" strategy. It is important to recognize a dominant dog for what it is and acknowledge that an uncontrolled child will do things that will be unacceptable to the dog, such as poking at its eyes, pulling its tail, hugging it, and so on. Appreciation of this potentially oil-and-water situation and knowledge of the circumstances that may lead to the expression of dominance-related aggression is invaluable in the management of these cases. The primary strategy for living in a home with a dominant dog and a child is to make sure that the dog and child are under control at all times when they are together. Sometimes it may be necessary to confine the dog to a crate, in which case the dog should have been previously trained to the crate. Another solution is to isolate the child from the dog by confining the child to a playpen or crib. If the child is under strict control and the dog is on lead or otherwise secured, no problems should arise. It is helpful to institute a dominance management program for the dog prior to the child's reaching toddling age—not that the child can participate, but firm control from the owners may help to defuse situations that portend conflict. These situations include competition over valued resources (the dog's food, toys, and bed or resting area), postural challenges (petting on the head, holding the muzzle, hugging, holding the dog's feet, pressure over the dog's spine), trying to make the dog do something it doesn't want to do, or admonishments. Unfortunately, children are unable to participate in dominance management programs until they are about six years old (perhaps a little earlier for a really smart youngster). It is my experience that between the ages of two and six, youngsters do not listen well and, in any case, have serious physical limitations when it comes to gaining the respect of a dominant dog. In extreme situations, in which a highly dominant and potentially aggressive dog is cohabiting with a persistent and invasive toddler, discretion may be the better part of valor. In such cases an alternative dwelling may have to be found for the dog, at least until the child is older.

If the unthinkable does happen and a child is bitten by a dominant dog, most owners report that the aggression was unprovoked. This is because they do not understand what is important to a dog—or what constitutes a threat or a challenge. To one versed in the ways of dominance, each event is highly predictable. One case I was consulted about recently, involving an Old English Sheepdog and a four-year-old girl, illustrates this point. The dog had been playing all day in the hot sun and decided to take a nap in the shade. The girl came up to the dog and went to hug it; it suddenly lunged toward her face. The result was a nasty bite, necessitating several stitches and causing considerable bruising and swelling. The owners thought that the dog's behavior was inexplicable and elected to have the dog euthanized immediately. The sad part is that the whole incident could have been avoided if only they had understood their dog. To the dog, being hugged was more of a challenge than a compliment, and challenging a tired, hot, dominant dog that is resting is asking for trouble. A dog of this temperament and a child of this age should have been supervised more carefully or, even better, kept apart. The first duty of dog owners is to know their dog and supervise it properly. Also, the parents of the little girl should probably have kept a closer eye on her. This incident was an unfortunate way to confirm the old adage that it is best to let sleeping dogs lie.

The final canine personality type that must be addressed in terms of possible negative interactions with children is that of the fearful dog. Once again, it is possible to spot these dogs by observing and assessing their reaction to strangers and their environment. A dog that backs up, balks, or hides when confronted by a stranger is probably a fearful dog. Likewise, a dog that is frightened of loud noises or that suffers from separation anxiety also falls into the fearful-personality category. Not all these dogs will be aggressive to children, but some will. Their early experiences have a great impact on how their fear is expressed. Fearful dogs generally do not direct their aggression toward family members and would not be expected to be a problem for the children of the household. Like dominant dogs, they usually pay no attention to young babies and will usually avoid an infant if they have any apprehension about it. When the baby gets older, however, and enters the terrible twos or the whirling-dervish period, the fearful dog may show some anxiety and attempt to keep a low profile when the going gets rough. Problems can occur if a dog like this is, for some reason, prevented from escaping—for example, if it is cornered. In such situations, the fearful dog may snap as a warning. Teeth marks on the forehead are, unfortunately, a common result of such encounters. Of course, when this happens, the child screams bloody murder, and worried parents scurry to the scene to admonish or punish the dog. While this reaction is understandable, it will do nothing to rectify the situation and may even make matters worse. What is required is for the owners to understand and monitor the developing situation and to deal with it proactively by intervening at the earliest possible opportunity if the dog appears anxious or is trying to get away. If the whirling-dervish period can be survived, the dog and child can become each other's best friend and can live together harmoniously. Fearful dogs particularly need a friend in this cruel world. The only ongoing problem that one might anticipate with a fearful dog would be aggression to the child's friends, especially those who are unfamiliar to the dog or ones who constantly intimidate the animal by being loud or invasive. Some of these child visitors will present a threat to the timorous canine, which, if approached or stared at by the child, may respond aggressively to drive the child away. A hands-off-the-dog policy is definitely in order here.

When it comes to fear, desensitization is central to treatment. Needless to say, it happens automatically with family members as the dog learns that it is not going to be hurt by a particular child, but the process can be actively sped along by engaging in desensitization exercises. Even if this doesn't prove necessary with family members, it is certainly helpful to desensitize the dog to your children's friends, as the process of acceptance can reduce the animal's fear of children in general. During desensitization, the dog is richly rewarded with food treats, praise, and petting for remaining calm when confronted with a low-intensity stimulus—for example, seeing the children at a distance. The intensity of the stimulus is then gradually increased (by bringing the children closer), with only good behavior being rewarded. Bad behavior should be ignored and the children reintroduced at a greater distance. Of course, it is important that the dog not be scared by the children during the retraining program. In this regard, it is most helpful to provide a safe haven for the dog that is off-limits to children. We all need a little retreat from the stresses and strains of everyday life, and for the dog a crate is an ideal denlike place. It is not even necessary to close the door on the crate; simply make it off-limits for the child and perhaps put it in some out-of-the-way place. The crate should be made welcoming by putting a blanket, toys, and perhaps food treats inside. It may also be helpful to feed the dog in the crate for a while to accelerate this acclimation. Eventually most dogs will learn to love the crate, as it provides sanctuary. When the child's friends come to visit they should be told each time that the crate is off-limits and that they should not approach, pet, or run after the dog. If such rules can be enforced, the chances of any problems will be considerably reduced. However, if there is any doubt that a child visitor is capable of following these instructions, the dog should be crated, put in another room, or put outside for the entire period of the child's visit.

In conclusion, both dominant and fearful dogs should be supervised properly in the presence of children and treated long-term by appropriate management to defuse the many potential problems. For predatory dogs, a little knowledge on the owner's part can go a long way toward preventing tragic accidents. There are a few dogs that should probably never be permitted to be around young children, but fortunately these dogs are few and far between and are not representative of the average family dog. As we saw in Samson's case, time, medical treatment, and behavioral modification therapy can usually restore a dog to its former status as man's best friend and a valued member of the family pack.

• TREATMENT FOR •

Aggression of Dogs Toward Babies

Dominant, fearful and predatory dogs may all present a threat to babies and young children if they are not properly controlled. Dominant dogs often do not pose a threat until children reach toddling age. Fearful dogs are most likely to be aggressive if they cannot escape the unwanted attentions of unfamiliar or seemingly obnoxious children. Predatory dogs may (rarely) pose a threat to newborn infants.

Prevention

1. Understand your dog and control your child.
2. Institute a dominance-management program for dominant dogs at the earliest opportunity. Do not allow young children and dominant dogs to be left alone together.
3. Fearful dogs will benefit from systematic desensitization exercises with other children to reduce their fear and apprehension. If there is any doubt about a fearful dog's trustworthiness around your child's friends, the dog should be isolated when they visit.
4. Predatory dogs should be carefully introduced to new babies. Do not leave such dogs alone with babies.

General Points

Before the baby arrives

1. Sharpen up on obedience training.
2. Make environmental changes early.
3. Take the dog for walks with the stroller.
4. Acclimate the dog to the diaper-changing routine using a doll.
5. Desensitize the dog to a tape recording of a baby crying.
6. Get behavior problems under control.
7. Bring home an article of the baby's clothing (not a diaper) from the hospital for the dog to smell.

After the baby arrives

1. Introduce the dog and the baby gradually, without a fuss, and with the dog on lead.
2. Do not ignore the dog in the presence of the baby.
3. Make sure that the dog and baby are always supervised when together.
4. Work to familiarize the dog with the baby and to acclimate it to the baby's ways as the child grows.
5. Watch for warning signs of dominance (such as growling) or fear (trying to run away or hide).
6. Never leave a predatory dog alone with a young baby.

PART II

The Fearful Dog

CHAPTER 6

The Dog Who Loved Too Much

Tennyson wrote that it is better to have loved and lost than never to have loved at all. Try explaining that to a dog with separation anxiety that is toughing it out alone following the departure of its beloved owners. About 4 percent of the 54 million dogs in the United States suffer from the wretched condition known as separation anxiety. In this condition, dogs become so closely bonded to their owners that they virtually have to be pried off them, and parting is not, as the saying goes, such sweet sorrow, but more of a living hell. Affected dogs are often gentle, doting, and sweet-natured, but the anxiety-related havoc they wreak in the owners' absence is sometimes misconstrued by the owners as being malicious, vindictive, or retributive. Some owners even spank their dogs on their return to punish them for their bad behavior, but this is both inappropriate and ineffective. Punishment never works if delivered more than a few seconds after an event; rather, it simply serves to confuse the already distraught and bewildered dog. Owners may swear that the dog knows what it has done because it "looks guilty," but the "guilt" is simply anticipation of punishment that the dog has learned to associate with the simultaneous presence of damaged property, the owner, and itself.

What would cause a dog to be this way? Is separation anxiety innate or acquired? Opinions vary, but the evidence overwhelmingly suggests that the dog suffering from separation anxiety is a product of its environment and is the canine equivalent of a dysfunctional person. These dogs appear to lack self-esteem and live vicariously through their owners, whom they adore and on whom they are totally dependent.

There is a famous story of a faithful English gun dog that was inadvertently locked in the parlor during its owners' prolonged absence. The dog did not eat any of the plentiful food surrounding it and died of starvation, obedient to the end. Although this is an inspiring, though pathetic, story of seeming altruism, and although one hates to speak ill of the dead, another explanation is equally moving but less magnanimous. It involves separation anxiety, a cardinal feature of which is anorexia—apparently to the bitter end. Many dogs with separation anxiety will not eat until their owners have returned; then, following a classically exuberant greeting ritual, they finally launch themselves at the still-full food bowl.

If this terrible anxiety and anorexia is environmentally induced, what factors determine it? Well, the jury is still out on that question, but it seems that psychological trauma in early puppyhood is largely to blame. Dogs with separation anxiety frequently have a history of being acquired from a pet store, from a pound, or from a person who didn't have a lot of time to spend with the dog. Although these dogs have not necessarily been beaten, they have been mistreated through isolation and neglect, and may have been separated from their mothers and littermates too early. Freud would probably have had a lot to say about this condition!

If you were to construct a scenario guaranteed to foster the development of separation anxiety, it would involve the impersonal rearing of batches of dogs in an environment where social contacts are scarce and close bonding with humans is virtually impossible. Many of the puppy mills of the Midwest provide examples of such environments. In such breeding farms, puppies are often separated from their mothers at the tender age of four or five weeks and are transported many miles to their final destination, the pet stores, where they are handled extensively, but only by an assortment of complete strangers. Pet-store dogs are usually sold when they are between three and five months of age, after they have spent months in isolation during a critical period of their social development. The product? Little Orphan Annie in a dog suit . . . an accident looking for a place to happen. If the new owners are kindly people, the dog will cling to them much the same as the proverbial drowning man will clutch at a straw, and, if permitted, a symbiotic bond will develop as post hoc evidence of an earlier abusive situation. I used to think that dogs with separation anxiety were always acquired at three or four months of age or later, but recently I have come across a few that were obtained much earlier, at eight or ten weeks. In all of these latter cases, the dogs had been weaned extremely early, which indicates that the trauma of early weaning alone can be enough to lay the groundwork for separation anxiety, at least in some cases.

Separation anxiety can be predicted with 100 percent accuracy in pound dogs, based on the reason the dog was brought to the pound, the pound attendant's impressions, and a simple test involving leaving the dog alone in the car for a few minutes and observing whether it barks or not. Significant findings in these areas indicate that a dog is likely to be prone to separation anxiety. However, the new owners are not exonerated from blame just because the dog is prone to the condition. Extremely empathetic owners seem to be much more likely to foster this problem in their dog. Susceptible dogs absorb all the attention and affection they are given and return it manyfold. They make wonderful pets, particularly for the emotionally needy person. In effect, the dog and owner become codependents and are virtually inseparable. But then there's the down side: these dogs simply can't cope on their own. It's as if every time the owner leaves, the dog thinks they've gone forever and starts to panic.

The diagnosis of separation anxiety is usually fairly straightforward. Owners call and report that their dog is destroying property in their home, but only in their absence. Doorways and windows—portals of exit and entry—are frequently targeted for destruction. It may be that the back of the door is scratched or that the molding around the door has been chewed; alternatively, window sills or blinds may come in for attack. This is due to what is called barrier frustration. Other factors contributing to the diagnosis include the classical history of a deprived puppyhood and extremely close attachment to the owner. Affected dogs follow their owners around the house so as not to let them out of their sight. They also sleep on or near their owners at night and will curl up next to them on the couch or drape themselves across their owner's feet when he or she is watching TV. Signs of distress, such as sad looks, cringing, or hiding, are usually obvious before the owner leaves, and whimpering or barking right after the owner has left is a hallmark of the condition. This vocalization usually occurs within ten to thirty minutes of the owner's departure. Owners are not always aware of this and may only find out about the ruckus from a neighbor. If they wait outside the door and listen, the dog may be on the inside listening to them! Sometimes it's necessary to make a tape recording to verify that whimpering and barking occur. As mentioned, affected dogs usually do not eat during their owner's absence. This is another cardinal sign of separation anxiety. Anxiety-related inappropriate elimination of urine and/or feces may occur during the owner's absence in extreme cases but is less common. The whole syndrome is topped off by exuberant greeting rituals that often continue for several minutes after the owner's arrival. Owners often interpret this behavior as a great compliment (which I suppose it is).

Elsa, a five-year-old neutered female Labrador Retriever mix, appeared to have a classical case of separation anxiety. Elsa's owners, Carl and Susan Blake, were the doting owners of this beautiful, sleek black creature. Elsa stayed very close to the Blakes as we entered the consulting room and took our seats. She was clearly stressed by the new environment and showed signs of anxiety, manifested as an inability to settle down and constant panting. She occasionally glanced sideways at her owners but showed absolutely no interest in me at all. I tried to coax her to me, but had no success. She preferred to remain close to Carl and Susan—safe and within petting distance. New things and new people were of no interest to Elsa, and I figured she would be a lot happier at home in her favorite chair, perhaps curled across Carl's lap. Salient features of Elsa's condition were destructive behavior in Carl and Susan's absence, trailing Carl or Susan around the house, anorexia when left alone, and elaborate greetings on her owners' return. The damage she inflicted on the home was pretty much confined to the areas around doors and windows. She had chewed the molding around the door, scratched up the rug, and destroyed one or two window blinds in her frenetic attempts to escape. The Blakes were beside themselves. How could such a wonderful, loving, otherwise well-balanced pet have such a distressing problem?

"Where did you get Elsa?" I asked Carl.

"We got her from a pound when she was a year old. She was cowering in a corner of her kennel. We felt so sorry for her . . . and we just couldn't resist those sad eyes."

I glanced at Elsa again. Sure enough, it would have been hard to resist that face, but their compassion had unwittingly contributed directly to the problem.

Carl went on, "We need to know up front—is this condition treatable?"

"Absolutely," I replied. "The odds are quite good that we can make a major improvement in Elsa's behavior, so that she is calm enough to tolerate your departures without showing these signs of anxiety. However, there are some things that I will have to ask you to do that I know you are going to find difficult."

Carl looked at me quizzically.

"Let's start with the easier stuff, such as changes in her management," I said. "First off, at least twenty or thirty minutes of aerobic exercise every day coupled with a low-protein diet will create a healthy balance between energy input and output. In addition, Elsa should be trained to obey one-word commands by working with her in five- or ten-minute training sessions twice daily. Your goal is to achieve a one hundred percent response, at least when there are no distractions around. Clear communication between you and her will help her know that you are in charge, and that will reduce her level of anxiety.

"Next, I'm afraid that you and Susan are both going to have to practice what I call independence training, which involves, for the short term at least, distancing yourself from Elsa to allow her to learn that she can survive without you. At present, she is so dependent on you that when you leave home, she panics, thinking that you have gone for good. Her negative early experiences have caused her to be this way, and it is important for you to teach her that she can, as it were, stand on her own four feet."

"How do we do that?" asked Susan.

"Okay," I said, "let's consider the nighttime aspects first. I see from the record that you are allowing Elsa to sleep on the bed with you at night, and although I have no objections to this for a normal, well-balanced dog, with Elsa, this is catering to her weakness. You should put a dog bed in the bedroom for her to sleep on. If she joins you in the night, take her gently by the collar or attach her lead, say 'Bed,' and lead her gently back to the dog bed. You must, of course, praise her the minute she is in the bed so that she knows that she has done the right thing. If this becomes too troublesome, try securing her lead to an immovable object, such as the leg of the dresser, so that she is physically prevented from reaching you. Some dogs get the message right away. Alternatively, a crate may be used to restrain her, but this must first be introduced to her during the day and in association with praise and treats. In this way, she will come to regard the crate as a haven and not a place of punishment. Some dogs will whine or carry on, at least for the first couple of nights. In such cases, it is most unwise to respond to her, which is essentially rewarding that behavior. Rather, it is best to direct her with a command. If worse comes to worst, you may have to try putting the crate outside the bedroom or downstairs. If she continues to bark, attend to her at progressively increasing intervals—first five minutes, then ten, fifteen, and up to twenty minutes. Give her firm directions such as 'Quiet' or 'Enough,' and praise her when she stops barking. It may take a night or two before she settles into the new routine.

"Also you have to teach her to be more independent during the day. Let's talk first about her continually following you around. She must be discouraged from doing this and should be taught to do something else instead, such as go to her bed and lie down. It's no good to tell her 'No' or say her name in an ominous tone and expect her to understand. This provides no direction for any dog, least of all one like Elsa, who is already confused and anxious. One trainer I know says that 'No' is used as a command so frequently that most dogs in this country think it is their first name. Also, if you keep using a dog's name as a command, eventually you won't even get its attention. It will assume you don't know what you want, so it will ignore you."

Carl, who was scribbling notes, looked up. I knew from his expression that the independence training was going to be difficult for him.

"Is there more?" he said a little anxiously.

"Yes, there is. You know how Elsa drapes herself across your feet or your lap when you watch television at night?"

"You mean that's not allowed either?" Carl asked.

"That's right," I replied, "at least not for the first three or four weeks. I would like you to tell her to go to her bed on the opposite side of the room or even in the kitchen. The point is that she should not be allowed to spend long hours in physical contact with you or Susan. She must learn to be independent—to stand up for herself. Call it confidence-building, if you will. It would also be helpful in training sessions to teach her to sit and stay while you move progressively farther away. You might eventually build up to being able to leave the room with her sitting in place. Then you can come back and praise her for obeying. These distancing techniques are all part of independence training and will help her to think for herself. You can even practice the sit-stay routine with her at the door, leaving for brief but progressively increasing periods of time."

"But every time I go toward the door she becomes extremely agitated. How can I prevent that?"

"You can desensitize her to what are known as predeparture cues," I replied. "She picks up on your every movement prior to your leaving. For example, if you grab your car keys, or your coat and hat, and make your way to the door, she'll get anxious right away. You should make a list of the things you do before you leave the house, including walking toward the door and reaching for the door handle. Run through the various actions in the evening in breaks between TV programs, but without actually leaving. You might, for example, grab your car keys or your coat, shuffle around, and then sit down again. She'll get up, think you are going to leave, become a little agitated, then realize it's a false alarm and settle down. If you practice this often enough, she will become desensitized to these signals, and you'll be able to approach the door more easily. Then you can graduate to touching the door, turning the doorknob, opening the door a crack, and so on."

"Okay," said Carl. "I have the independence training bit down, and I understand you want me to work on predeparture cues. Is there anything else I should be doing?"

"Yes. You should both ignore her for twenty minutes before you leave and after you return."

"You mean *totally* ignore her?" he questioned.

"Yes, totally," I replied. "You should not look at her, touch her, or speak to her during this period. You should walk around her if she is in your way and in general pretend that she just doesn't exist."

"What's the purpose of that?" Carl asked.

"It will help to even out the emotional crests and troughs in her day," I explained. "I have some personal experience with this, as my daughter, Keisha, suffered from a degree of separation anxiety at one time—perhaps brought on by her brief but unpleasant experiences in day care. I observed that if her mother made a tremendous fuss over her before leaving, saying things like, 'I'll be back soon, don't you worry. Mommy's only going to be away for a short time,' she became worse. The more her mother attempted to reassure her, the more anxious Keisha became. She would sometimes even start sobbing and crying inconsolably. On the other hand, if her mother sneaked out unobserved, the problem of her being away was not such a big one for Keisha to handle. What I learned to do was to distract Keisha in the next room by engaging her in some activity such as coloring, while my wife surreptitiously departed. Eventually Keisha would ask, 'Where's Mommy?' and I would simply say, 'She's gone out on an errand,' to which she would reply, 'Oh,' and that was it. Before we started this behavior modification, there was a lot of hugging and kissing on Mom's return, as this was the high spot in Keisha's day. This had to be tuned down too.

"Low-key departures and arrivals were certainly helpful in resolving Keisha's distress, and the same strategy appears to benefit dogs that are prone to separation anxiety." I explained that in one experimental series, a mild case of canine separation anxiety resolved spontaneously because of something the owner had done (or rather had not done). The dog's owner had come up with the idea of slipping out of the house unnoticed, so as to avoid emotional departures. This was all that was necessary to correct the problem. Minimizing fuss on exit and entry appears to be a powerful tool for the treatment of separation anxiety.

Then I used yet another real-life example of separation anxiety to bring home to the Blakes the normalizing effects of attention withdrawal. It was a rather extreme case in which the distraught owner of a dog with separation anxiety informed me that when his dog destroyed a two-thousand-dollar stereo speaker, he had finally decided that euthanasia was the only solution. Having made this decision, he could no longer bear to look at the dog or interact with it because he felt so guilty. The day before he was due to have the dog put to sleep, someone told him to contact me as a last resort, and he dutifully came. As it turns out, from the time he had started to ignore the dog, there had been no further instances of destruction. He interpreted this as the dog's knowing what was going to befall him. Rather, the dog's response was testimony to the powerful effect of complete attention withdrawal.

When faced with this solution to the problem of separation anxiety, most owners say, "What's the point of owning the dog if I can't interact with it?" But actually you can—*just not to the same extent.* Although some behaviorists implement fairly austere programs of complete avoidance, most, like myself, advocate a less extreme approach in which independence is encouraged in the manner described above.

"Finally," I told Carl, "you should attempt to pair your departures with some pleasant experience for Elsa. This is a technique referred to as counterconditioning. Presently, Elsa is conditioned to anticipate anxiety and misery on your departure. We would like to turn that around so that she may even look forward to your departure. Let's start with food."

For dogs that are food-oriented—so-called chow hounds (which Elsa was)—food is normally the stimulus of choice. Unfortunately, most treats don't last long enough to hold the dog's interest when you're gone and will be wolfed down before you leave. However, if you put the food down as you leave you are running into the anorexic period—quite a problem. One way around this is to give the dog something, such as a large bone, that can provide an hour and a half or more of gastronomic delight, twenty minutes before you leave. This will span the critical time period preceding and immediately following your departure. The bone should be uncooked to prevent it from shattering into sharp fragments, which could cause the dog intestinal problems of one sort or another; raw bones (which are what wild dogs consume, of course) present no problem at all, as the bone dissolves in the strong acid of the stomach. Another slightly cleaner version of this same strategy is the use of a presterilized bone, which can be purchased from a pet store. Like all long bones, they have a hollow marrow cavity down the middle, which should be packed with peanut butter or cheese spread to maintain the dog's attention. It is difficult for a dog to finish this kind of treat quickly; however, one dog I know learned to clean out the marrow cavity in eight minutes flat by sucking the cheese out! Nylon bones can be drilled with holes that are then filled with the same gooey food as the presterilized bone, producing the same effect. Alternatively, a Kong rubber chew toy, which is hollow, can be packed with food to make it more attractive. Use several of these long-acting food treats at a time . . . why stop at one?

The last measure I discussed with the Blakes was the daytime use of a crate. Dogs with separation anxiety that have not been acclimated to a crate do not take kindly to this confinement in the owner's absence—and that is an understatement! I have heard of situations in which dogs have broken their teeth and nails on the wire cage sides and the owners have come home to find their dog collapsed in a pool of blood, exhausted. Luckily, Elsa already had a crate in which she was fairly happy. A blanket was placed inside the crate for added comfort, and she was fed in there sometimes. Whenever she went inside the crate she was praised and given food treats, and the door was almost never locked. I asked the Blakes to incorporate the crate as a restraining device during their periods of absence, explaining to them that a dog enclosed in a solid-sided crate may feel more secure than when in a large open area. The Blakes agreed to try out the crate during short absences.

As a monitoring technique, I suggested that they record with a tape recorder any sounds that Elsa might make following their departure. This, I thought, would be a more accurate indicator of the success of treatment than simply noting whether damage had occurred or not. I also explained that making a tape recording of household sounds and playing it while they were away might also be of some benefit, as it would break the silence of her solitude. (Some behaviorists recommend leaving the radio or television on, but I have not found either of these strategies particularly useful.)

Finally, although I assured the Blakes that they would have some success with this treatment program, I offered to prescribe medication to reduce Elsa's fear and anxiety. They agreed to this supportive measure, and Elsa was started on an antidepressant called amitriptyline. Although there are many different medications that may help dogs with separation anxiety, amitriptyline is the gold standard, being effective in the majority of cases. It has the added advantages of being inexpensive and, if used properly, relatively free from side effects.

The Blakes called me back after four weeks to report some success (they estimated a 50 percent improvement), but not a complete cure. I was considering whether to increase the dose of the medication, but Carl had another idea. He had devised a sound-activated tape recorder that played a taped message of himself giving Elsa directions and praise. The idea was that if Elsa barked while he was away, the tape recorder would automatically turn on and deliver brief messages such as "Lie down, Elsa. Lie down. . . . That's a good dog. Good girl, Elsa." The device was ingenious. It employed a tape loop, an inexpensive tape recorder, and some special circuitry that he had designed. (Little did I know that Carl's occupation was developing new electronic circuitry for a well-known defense contractor that manufactured missiles—he was the proverbial rocket scientist!) For him this clever device was simply a lunch-break project, but for me it represented a breakthrough in dealing with these cases. During the week that followed, he set up a video camera and filmed Elsa's reaction to the device while she was left alone. The effect was most impressive. Every time Elsa got up and barked, Carl's voice would kick in. Elsa looked a little confused at first, but then followed the command and would lie down. While under voice control in this way, her apprehension seemed to be considerably reduced, and she would remain quiet for quite some time before standing, retriggering the machine, and going through the sequence again.

Following a two-week trial period, Elsa was about 90 percent improved, but Carl still noted some apprehension on her part and, being a perfectionist, wanted to struggle for a more complete cure.

He requested that I try Elsa on a different medication, for a trial period at least. I opted for the human antianxiety medication alprazolam. Alprazolam (Xanax) is a benzodiazepine tranquilizer. This group of drugs, which includes diazepam (Valium), seems to be extremely effective in controlling animal anxiety, as shown by its ability to control the anxious vocalizations of rat pups temporarily separated from their mothers. I thought that maybe alprazolam may help Elsa. After a few trial administrations of alprazolam to Elsa to get the dose adjusted correctly, the moment of truth arrived: Elsa was given the drug and left alone for a whole day. Needless to say, Carl had his tape recorder and a video camera rolling. The results were spectacular. Elsa did not mind their getting ready to leave, and showed no signs of anxiety whatsoever. When the Blakes left, Elsa simply went across to her couch, curled up, and slept. Eventually, she even gave this up and just lay at a chosen spot on the floor. She would greet them in a warm and friendly way on their return, but not exuberantly, and to all intents and purposes was completely cured.

Carl was ecstatic, and I was also delighted. He deserved this kind of result, having put in the effort he did and having gone through the ordeals of the preceding weeks. Once Elsa had grown accustomed to being alone, the dose of medication was gradually reduced until she could be left alone without medication. The weaning process went well, and Elsa recovered to apparent normalcy. The Blakes would return to a calm, contented dog and an intact home. With dog and owner happy, this case seemed to be solved.

There was a postscript to this story, however. Several months later, Carl called me to report that Elsa had relapsed during a thunderstorm. I had made a note when I first saw Elsa that she was frightened of thunderstorms; this was no particular surprise, as this fear often accompanies separation anxiety. Apparently Elsa had been alone when a particularly violent storm passed through the area. The combination of separation anxiety (albeit controlled) and thunderstorm phobia was more than she could handle, and it was pretty much back to the beginning in terms of treatment. At last report, Elsa had once made steady improvement in her separation anxiety, but remained uneasy during storms. Carl was still happy, though, as Elsa, the dog who loved too much, was so much better than she had been. Carl still uses his device sometimes, and recently he and I have been talking about making it more generally available. It seems a shame not to share the discovery. Now if only we could come up with a device that would help dogs during thunderstorms, we would really be in business.

• TREATMENT FOR •

Separation Anxiety

Dogs with separation anxiety often have a dysfunctional history. Because they are insecure, they tend to follow their owners around the house, look anxious as the owners prepare to leave, and become distraught when they are finally alone. They bark and whine immediately after their owners leave and often destroy things, particularly moldings around windows and doors. Temporary anorexia during the owners' absence is another feature and, in some extreme cases, the anxiety may cause dogs to urinate or defecate when their owners are away. An exuberant greeting ritual completes the syndrome.

Treatment

1. Try a program of desensitization and counterconditioning.
2. Begin a program of independence training.
3. Ignore the dog for twenty minutes before leaving and on returning.
4. Employ sustained release food treat 20 minutes before departure.
5. If prescribed, medicate the dog with antianxiety drugs or antidepressants.

Footnote: Owners can compound their dog's separation anxiety by empathizing too much. Firm but supportive leadership, providing clear direction, can go a long way toward reconciling this behavioral problem.

CHAPTER 7

Thunderstruck

A t times, the forces of nature act with such intensity that we are virtually compelled to suspend our normal activities and gaze in awe. There is something exciting, almost frightening, about witnessing nature at work during a storm as the trees bend like reeds, lightning forks from the sky, and peals of thunder reverberate around the heavens. If people are so profoundly affected by thunderstorms, then what about animals? Are they affected, too? As it turns out, they are—to varying degrees ranging from mild arousal to frank fear. Many dogs are perturbed by thunderstorms, but only a few go on to develop thunderstorm phobia. The reaction of phobic dogs is rather extreme, leaving the owner in no doubt that their dog views the storm as some kind of apocalypse. Affected dogs relentlessly seek the attention of their owners or some safe place and puff and pant as they pace to and fro, sometimes losing control of their bladder or bowels in their anxiety. If the owners of such a dog happen to be away during the storm, the animal's attempts to escape the terror and be with them are often expressed as barrier frustration (as also occurs in separation anxiety). In extreme cases, dogs have been known to tear through screens and hurl themselves out of windows, sustaining serious injuries.

Certain breeds are more likely to suffer from thunderstorm phobia than others. Northern breeds, such as Huskies and Samoyeds, and some larger breeds, such as Labradors, Retrievers, and German Shepherds, seem particularly prone. This apparent breed specificity may indicate that some genetic factors are involved in the condition, but differences in management may also account for the bias. After all, it's a lot easier for the owner of a Lhasa Apso to pick it up and cradle it in his arms during a storm than it is for someone who owns a Labrador. Dogs with thunderstorm phobia are often anxious in other situations as well, so it appears that thunderstorm phobia is sometimes an exaggerated component of a more generalized anxiety disorder. Owners frequently report that their dog was mildly anxious during storms starting when it was a few months old, but that the condition suddenly worsened in midlife following a particularly violent storm. Although the demographics and development of thunderstorm phobia in dogs are well known to behavioral practitioners, nobody really knows for sure why particular breeds have a predilection to it or why the full-blown condition often takes years to develop. At this point, any suggestions are purely speculative, and the true story may not be revealed for some time.

A year or so ago, a client called me to find out why her dog had suddenly developed a fear of thunderstorms, and wanted to know what could be done. Before I got on with the usual round of questions, I decided to try my luck with a little guessing game.

"Is your dog seven years old?" I asked nonchalantly.

"He is," she said, a little surprised at my apparent clairvoyance. "How did you know?"

"Is he a . . . Labrador?" I ventured.

"Yes, he is a Lab," she gasped. "This is uncanny."

I was on a roll, so I had to have one final guess.

"He's black, isn't he?" I said.

"He *is* black. This is unbelievable. How do you do this? How can you tell me over the telephone what age and breed and color my dog is?"

I quickly put the woman out of her misery by explaining that the guess about age of onset was an average figure, that the breed was a three-to-one shot, and the color was a two-to-one venture. I had just been lucky. Nevertheless, she understood the significance of my remarks: that we were dealing with a well-defined and fairly common syndrome.

Thunderstorm phobia is a relatively common phobia that I classify in the "inanimate fear" category. This category includes fear of sights, sounds, and smells, but fear of sounds is by far the most common. Thunderstorm phobia itself has been labeled as sound phobia, for what may seem like obvious reasons. However, there are many other components of storms besides thunder that will generate fear by themselves, such as wind noise, the sound of rain falling, and darkening skies.

An eminent behaviorist told me there are two sound-related theories that are under investigation to explain why dogs develop thunderstorm phobia. One theory purports that affected dogs have subnormal hearing and become alarmed when the mighty sound of thunder penetrates their relatively silent world. Advocates of the muted-hearing theory are testing the hearing acuity of thunderstorm-phobic dogs across the sound spectrum using complicated electrophysiological methods. I find this theory difficult to accept, because all the thunderstorm-phobic dogs I have seen appear to hear very well. The other hypothesis suggests the opposite, that thunderstorm-phobic dogs have extremely acute hearing, to the point that the sound of thunder may cause discomfort or pain. I have a hard time with this theory as well, as I once treated three thunderstorm-phobic dogs that would curl up in front of a drum set and sleep peacefully while the owner's teenage son was pounding the skins. Sound-sensitive? I don't think so.

The question is, if the dog's hearing is normal, why would thunder be such a problem? It could be that, as with humans, it is the whole ambience of the storm that generates fear, and that thunder is just one component of the whole experience. Stretching this argument a little further, it could even be that thunder, like wind, rain, and darkening skies, is a neutral stimulus that has become paired with some other aversive event occurring during the storm. In apparent contradiction to this hypothesis, however, owners sometimes report that their thunderstorm-phobic dogs are also frightened of other sounds, such as cars backfiring or loud street construction. These owners feel that the coexistence of multiple sound phobias confirms their dog's sound sensitivity. However, all the dogs I have seen developed thunderstorm phobia before they developed their sensitivity to other sounds; without much of a stretch of the imagination, most of these other sounds sound like thunder. Elementary sound phobia, originating purely in response to sounds, does exist, but is not necessarily associated with thunderstorm phobia. I have encountered dogs that are petrified of gunshots but couldn't care less about a thunderstorm. The opposite is also true, that thunderstorm-phobic dogs may not necessarily be frightened of gunshots or fireworks. Once again, it is difficult to know for sure exactly what is going on with these dogs.

Because of my great interest in thunderstorm phobia, I am always pleased to see new cases and find out how well they conform to the stereotype. When I take a dog's history, I always feel I might stumble across some additional pieces of information that might lead to a better understanding of the condition. With this in mind, I always take a detailed behavioral history and try to phrase my questions to be open-ended so as not to influence the answer. One case I saw a few years ago was particularly memorable, as some of the information the owner provided to me during the interview process seeded ideas that led me to develop a new approach to the understanding of this condition. The patient in question was a seven-year-old spayed female German Shepherd called Sybil. I could tell from the outset that her owner, Laureen Jackson, would have done anything to help her dog, which to her was something of a surrogate child. Laureen described Sybil's condition as an extreme phobia of many weather conditions, including thunderstorms, wind, sleet, and snow. She also added that Sybil was frightened of the sound of airplanes and quarry blasting. Laureen first realized that Sybil had a problem with storms when the dog was only seven months old. At this time, Sybil's sound phobia was confined to thunderstorms; the other sound phobias appeared over the years. I was intrigued to learn that Sybil had also shown signs of separation anxiety as a youngster and was a little cautious around strangers. With this triad of fears—of people, of things, and of situations—Sybil had a full house.

Sybil's thunderstorm phobia had reached its acme the previous summer, when Laureen moved to a new house. What had been a low-grade phobia escalated by several orders of magnitude following the move. The new house was situated on the top of a windy hill and had a particular type of fluted roof tile and overhanging eaves that together somehow caused peculiar howling sounds, particularly when a northeaster was blowing. Laureen credited the sudden deterioration in Sybil's condition to this acoustic phenomenon. I could see that Sybil was in a sorry state; even the visit to my consulting room had stressed her to the limit. She was salivating, panting, and pacing throughout the interview, almost as if in the midst of a storm. She showed some mild interest in me and was, if anything, on the friendly side, but Laureen was clearly the center of her universe. Sybil was sensitive to her every gesture and was constantly trying to catch her eye, sometimes standing in front of her and pawing at her gently, looking for any kind of acknowledgment.

Laureen reported that Sybil's behavior during thunderstorms was becoming progressively more extreme. Several hours before a storm, Sybil would begin continuous pacing, panting, and whining, and would refuse to be separated from Laureen. By the time the storm actually arrived, Sybil was hysterical and, in addition to the above behavior, would salivate profusely and sometimes vomit or urinate on the floor. This represents a fairly severe form of the thunderstorm phobia disorder. During one of the storms, Laureen had tried isolating Sybil from the sight and sound of the storm by confining her in a large pen in the cellar. She stayed down there with the dog, but had to leave for a short while during the storm to attend to some business. During her absence, she left a radio on to console Sybil and drown out the faint sound of thunder. On her return, she found a scene reminiscent of a chainsaw massacre. Sybil had broken off her toenails by scratching the concrete floor and had bent the bars of the pen with her teeth. With her gums and nailbeds bleeding profusely, she had then escaped into the room and resumed her frenzied pacing and scratching, leaving a trail of blood wherever she went. On another occasion, a storm came out of nowhere while Sybil was alone in the house. In her frenzy, Sybil destroyed a cherrywood door and the surrounding wall, inflicting some two thousand dollars' worth of damage. These last two events were what had precipitated Laureen's visit to our clinic.

Laureen had tried many preventive measures prior to seeking me out. She had tried scolding Sybil, which only seemed to make the anxiety worse. She had tried keeping her in a windowless cellar, both crated and uncrated, and had tried two different tranquilizers at her vet's suggestion, but neither was effective, and one made Sybil extremely wobbly on her legs. The only thing that seemed to help Sybil at all was to be downstairs and very close to Laureen. Even on nights that weren't stormy, Sybil would pace and whine in the bedroom upstairs every night until Laureen went down to the cellar to sleep with her. Presumably Sybil wasn't about to take any chances. Laureen had given up resisting and had taken to sleeping downstairs on a couch in the cellar with Sybil's lead in her hand. Although this strategy seemed to provide Sybil with some relief, it did not ride well with Laureen's husband, who, at the time of the behavioral interview, had not seen much of his wife at night for six months or so.

One interesting observation that Laureen shared with me related to some other behavior Sybil exhibited during storms, aside from the panting, pacing, and attention seeking. Apparently Sybil had a penchant for trying to get into the sink, bath, or shower stall during the storm. Laureen asked me whether I had an explanation for this curious behavior. Although I briefly discussed denning and the canine propensity to seek out small, enclosed spaces in a crisis, I did not really believe that this was the whole story. I registered the eccentric behavior as food for thought and proceeded to elaborate a treatment plan for Sybil.

Treatment of fears and phobias is normally accomplished by careful reintroduction to the fear-inducing stimulus, which in the case of thunderstorm phobia is, supposedly, storm sounds, particularly the sound of thunder itself. Tape recordings of storm sounds can be made by owners, or audiotapes or CDs featuring storm sounds (plus or minus music) can be purchased from stores. Whatever the source, the recording has to be good enough to fool the dog and should be checked initially to make sure that it does elicit a fearful response. The whole desensitization exercise is a waste of time if the sound recording does not generate a phobic response. Behavior-modification sessions begin by training the dog to tolerate exposure to thunderstorm sounds at a low volume. This is accomplished by playing a favorite game with the dog or training the dog to sit (and stay) for food rewards during exposure to the sound at, say, level one on the stereo. When the dog is no longer concerned about the sound at that level, the volume is cranked up a notch and the procedure is repeated, and so on. At each stage of the procedure, the dog is rewarded for remaining calm and under control. One important point is that the dog should not be exposed to the full-intensity stimulus at any time during the retraining process, or else progress made to that point will be forfeited. Unfortunately, this also means that the dog should be prevented from experiencing real storms during the desensitization program. For this reason, desensitization programs are only effective during the storm-free season of the year. Luckily, it was approaching that time of the year, so I launched Laureen on this program. I stressed the importance of preventing Sybil from becoming anxious or fearful at any stage of the program and advised Laureen to be patient and to content herself with slow progress through the various treatment phases. At the slightest sign of balking, she was to reduce the volume to the previous level and proceed as before. Another important detail of the program to which I drew Laureen's attention was that training should be conducted in several different areas of the house to prevent what is called localized learning. As odd as it may seem, a dog that is desensitized in only one area of the house may still be fearful if it is exposed to a fear-inducing stimulus in other locations.

Before leaving the subject of behavior-modification therapy, I left Laureen with a few words of advice about what to do in the event of an actual storm (the weather is particularly unreliable in New England, and there can sometimes be thunderstorms even in the middle of January). I was particularly concerned about the signals that she might be transmitting to Sybil during a storm. In essence, I advised that she should radiate confidence, not concern, and should attempt to divert Sybil's attention from the storm by strong leadership. If an owner shows concern during a storm, even if that concern is for the dog's well-being, the dog will pick up on this and become even more anxious. Telling a dog that's anxious that everything is okay and praising and petting it are the worst things to do. It is far better to give the dog some clear direction, telling it to come or sit, or perhaps attempting to engage it in a game of some sort, than to attempt to comfort the distraught animal. If a dog sees you are not worried, it will gain confidence itself, fortified by its intrepid leader. In addition, I asked Laureen to concentrate on confidence-building exercises for Sybil between storms (such as tug-of-war, allowing the dog to win) and advised her to treat Sybil in a more matter-of-fact way. I predicted that if Laureen was able to master all the facets of the desensitization program and to radiate confidence in her interactions with Sybil, she could make some reasonable improvement in Sybil's general condition, at least until the thunderstorm season arrived.

At this point in the interview I took time out to explain the main weakness of the desensitization program in treating thunderstorm phobia: relapse. Although a dog may become able to endure almost deafening levels of storm sounds during training sessions, when the real storm arrives there is a good chance that the severely phobic dog will revert back to its old behavior and all the good work will be undone. I have spoken to several other behaviorists on this matter, and they all agree that although desensitization programs are extremely effective for treating most other types of fear, severe thunderstorm phobia seems to be resistant to treatment by desensitization alone. This leads me to suspect that there is something else going on in this condition. One of the experts I talked to said he felt that changes in atmospheric pressure were involved. This is not an unreasonable suggestion, and would explain the dog's ability to pick up on an impending storm well before its arrival. Some dogs will start to pant or pace hours before a storm actually arrives, when to our senses there is nothing going on climatically. This apparent canine clairvoyance may have something to do with barometric pressure or some other factors, but may also be a function of the dog's superior sensory ability.

Because of my lack of complete faith in the effectiveness of desensitization strategies alone for treatment of this condition, and because of the severity of Sybil's condition, I decided to recommend pharmacological treatment in addition to behavior-modification therapy. The medication I chose, buspirone, is a potent anxiety-reducing drug—one of a new breed of "smart drugs." Smart drugs are called that because they target specific receptors in the brain and produce relatively pure behavioral effects with minimal side effects. I had some good previous experiences using buspirone in the treatment of thunderstorm phobia, including my first medically treated thunderstorm case ever, which almost completely resolved on medication alone. I was a little concerned about the cost of treatment, as it can be quite expensive for a dog as big as Sybil, but apparently this was not a problem for Laureen. She agreed to this adjunctive medical treatment, and Sybil was started on a relatively low dose of buspirone. I cautioned that the full effects of the drug would not become apparent for a week or two at least, and advised Laureen to stay in touch on a regular basis.

I next spoke to her a week later, when she reported some slight improvement in Sybil's condition. She described Sybil as being less skittish around the house and apparently not alarmed by things that would otherwise have scared her. The weather had not been good during the week since our appointment, with heavy rain and gusting winds, and this had caused Sybil to engage in some lengthy bouts of barking, one of them lasting forty minutes. The mild improvement reported, however, made me feel that things were moving in the right direction, and in any case, the effects of the medication were still building. A week later, Laureen's report was glowing. Now Sybil was not bothered by airplanes or moderate wind noise, although strong winds were still a problem. Laureen had been able to sleep upstairs for the first time in six months, and her husband was delighted. It seemed that we were definitely on the right track.

Progress over the next several weeks was a little checkered, with some setbacks during some late season thunderstorms, but there were also some very good periods in which Sybil was much calmer and more laid-back than she had ever been. During one of the storms, though, Sybil was reported to have jumped into the sink again and then leaped onto the top of the washing machine and dryer before ending up in the bathtub. I still didn't know what to make of this behavior, although I ruminated on it some more.

Some weeks later, after an increase in the medication dose and continued advice about handling during storms, Sybil became a different dog. She would play with her tennis ball during a storm, and wind noise and rain were no longer a problem. We were all delighted with Sybil's progress, but just as I was beginning to savor the fruits of victory, Sybil relapsed during a particularly violent thunderstorm. She had not been nervous as the storm approached and appeared happy and relaxed as distant thunder rolled, but she fell to pieces when there was a loud crack of thunder right over the house, and she ran to her owner, panting. Laureen took her down to the cellar immediately and went through the usual routines. Although Sybil was obviously distraught, she was more manageable than she had been prior to treatment, being able to accept food treats and occasionally showing some interest in her tennis ball. Despite this setback, there was no doubt that Sybil was much improved, and Laureen was pleased with her progress. This case taught me a lot but also left me with more questions. There seemed to be other factors operating that I just didn't know about.

At a meeting some time after this, I spoke to a colleague who was in the process of conducting some research into thunderstorm phobia using a thunderstorm simulation tank. I took the opportunity to see if I could learn anything more about the treatment of thunderstorm phobia. As time was at a premium, I was fairly direct in my line of questioning.

"If you are presented with a dog with severe thunderstorm phobia and there are no holds barred in terms of treatment, can you
cure that dog?"

She thought for a while and then replied, "No, I'm afraid I can't."

I felt some vindication at this response. I was not alone. Although I felt I could improve affected dogs considerably, I was not
able to effect a complete cure, at least in the most severe cases.

As the weeks and months went by, I continued to see cases of
thunderstorm phobia and to delve into these dogs' clinical histories. The histories corroborated my previously held views on these
dogs' ability to hear and their lack of sound sensitivity, but I also
began to notice a recurrent theme of fascination with sinks, show-
ers, Jacuzzis, baths, and other spots that had something to do with
water. It seemed that during storms, affected dogs turn into canine
divining rods, seeking out water in any of the locations it is normally found in houses. There is no other fear-inducing condition I
know that generates this response. So why thunderstorms? Why
would a ninety-pound German Shepherd go out of its way to sit in
the bathroom sink during a thunderstorm? Quite apart from anything else, it sure looks odd. Not every thunderstorm-phobic dog
leaps onto the appliances, however; some of them merely seek out
the bathroom. Others squeeze behind the pipes feeding the toilet
tank, and in one case a woman reported that her dog went out into
the garden, where it would stand up to its ankles in water in her
child's play pool. I mused about this phenomenon for some time
and then finally called a veterinarian friend of mine, Morgan Long,
for a little targeted advice. Morgan, you see, is a whiz where things
electrical are concerned, and I was beginning to think that electricity might be involved somehow.

"What's going on with these dogs, Morgan?" I asked him. "Why would a thunderstorm-phobic dog seek out water or a bathroom appliance during a storm?"

"Have you ever considered the electrical properties of these things?" he asked me.

"Not really," I had to confess.

"A sink, for example," he went on, "is normally supplied by metal pipes and, therefore, acts as an electrical grounding device. It is probably one of the best grounds in the house," he added for good measure. "A dog coming into contact with metallic sink fixtures, including the pipe, would ground itself to the earth, releasing any static electrical charge."

"I see," I mused. "What you're saying is that a dog would be able to prevent the buildup of static charge by staying in contact with one of these fixtures."

"Precisely," he chirped. "Think about the shocks you sometimes get when you get out of your car and touch the door handle—the car is charged, and, depending on the type of shoes you're wearing, you can become a conductor to the ground. You can get quite a zap. If you were riding along in the kitchen sink instead of a car, you wouldn't have that problem," he said drolly. Then he added, "As a matter of fact, I think the reason some dogs are frightened of traveling in the car is that they get shocks when they get out. I have had some owners put antistatic drag strips on the back of their cars to treat their dog's fear of car travel and about half of these dogs have improved dramatically."

"Wow," I said. "You should publish this and let a few other people know about it. It really seems like a good idea. But back to the thunderstorm-phobic dogs. I guess they would pick up a static charge only if they were insulated from the surface they were walking on."

"That's true," said Morgan. "Their foot pads *are* fairly good electrical resistors, and some floors are poor conductors too."

"Maybe we should be spraying their feet with antistatic spray," I quipped. Then it dawned on me that this wasn't such a bad idea.

"How about putting thunderstorm-phobic dogs on a conducting floor?" Morgan said. "Maybe a wet one."

"Or putting a choke chain around their neck and letting one end trail on the floor to release the static charge?" I added.

"Any or all of the above," said Morgan.

We talked excitedly for several more minutes and wondered how we could ever substantiate the new theory. Could we charge dogs up with static electricity and see if they became anxious? Such a thing seemed almost impossible to arrange, even after extensive conversations with the folks at MIT. Alternatively, could we learn anything by preventing the buildup of static electricity in thunderstorm-phobic dogs and seeing if they responded differently? The latter question could probably not be answered immediately, however, as it would take time for dogs to get used to the idea that storms and all the related secondary phenomena were no longer associated with an unpleasant experience. Theoretically, this would take about as long as a successful desensitization program in the storm-free season.

As we considered this theory, still other questions arose. Was the buildup of static electricity intrinsically unpleasant? Or was the problem a result of the dog's receiving periodic electric shocks during a storm? Neither of us could figure out the answers to these questions, and we weren't sure how to find out. I did call Laureen, though, and asked her about the flooring in her house. What she told me was compatible with the developing theory. Her previous home was mostly uncarpeted, and presumably the floors were electrically conductive, whereas in her new home there was wall-to-wall carpet upstairs, quarry tile on the ground floor, and concrete in the cellar. If buildup of static electricity was a factor, it would not be surprising that Sybil developed a particular aversion for the second floor of her new home.

The enigma of thunderstorm phobia continued to haunt me as the weeks went by. Then, one day during a visit to the Museum of Science in Boston, I took my children to see the lightning show. This show is a spectacular performance put on partly to entertain visitors to the museum but also to educate them about electricity and lightning. At the center of the show is the original Van de Graaff generator, designed and built by Van de Graaff himself. This gargantuan generator stands some eighty feet high and consists of large and small metal-clad spheres supported on columns. It was originally used to generate millions of volts of static electricity for the manufacture of isotopes used in cancer treatment. The generator now stands in a specially prepared amphitheater at the Museum of Science and, among other things, is a monument to earlier scientific pioneers. My children and I watched in awe as the presenter caused electricity to arc between the huge spheres and smaller ones, resulting in loud cracks of "thunder." A wonderful lecture accompanied the display, which was conducted inside a large bird-cagelike structure (a Faraday cage) for the safety of the onlookers. After the demonstration, I approached the presenter, Ken Pauley, and spoke to him for several minutes about electrical fields and static electricity. I also mentioned the reason for my curiosity. He was extremely helpful and said he would assist me with my project. Needless to say, I took him up on his kind invitation, and a few days later I told him the full story of the dogs and the static-electricity theory. He said that if the Museum of Science would give him approval, he would be happy to work with me on arranging an experiment involving the generator. Our plan basically involved bringing some thunderstorm-phobic dogs to the Van de Graaff generator—inside the Faraday cage—and filming them to record any reaction they might show on entering the electrical field. Needless to say, I planned to be with the dogs at the time, as I wouldn't subject a dog to anything that I wasn't prepared to experience myself. This would also allow me to record the dogs' heart rate and respiratory rate as more objective measures of a fearful response.

It was first necessary for me to draw up a protocol and submit it to the officials at the Museum of Science. I also had to draw up a satisfactory consent form that owners would sign to give us permission to use their dogs for the study. All this was completed in record-breaking time, and it wasn't too long before I set off with camera in hand to meet my first volunteer patient and anxious owner in the foyer of the Museum of Science at seven o'clock one morning. I also arranged for my friend and colleague from the Tufts medical school, Dr. Lou Shuster, to meet us there. Lou was really interested in the project and was looking forward to helping collect the data.

Ken led us down to the dimly lit amphitheater and, after climbing into the control cockpit, activated the rotors within the spheres to start the electrons flowing. The first time around, he did not insulate the spheres from the ground, so no static charge built up. This was basically a dry run, or control period, during which we could assess the dog's reaction to the surroundings and background noise without the static component present. The result, during the dry run phase, was that the dog's behavior did not change; there was also no change in its heart rate or respiratory rate. After a brief rest, we repeated the procedure, but this time the static field was allowed to build up to around 400,000 volts. I could feel the effects of the electrical field myself, but I can't say that they were unpleasant. I felt a little prickly, and my hair stood on end all over my head, making me look like a sunflower. Suddenly it struck me how bizarre the whole setup must have appeared to an onlooker. Here was the proverbial mad scientist and a dog being exposed to close to half a million volts of static electricity inside an oversized birdcage. It really did look like a scene from *Dr. Who* rather than the serious science project that it was intended to be.

Although the dog balked on entering the electrical field, it did not indulge in a full thunderstorm frenzy with pacing and panting. The fact that he balked meant that he sensed the electrical field, but instead of becoming more apprehensive, he seemed to calm down. It was really puzzling. At least we had shown that simply being exposed to the electric field was not an aversive experience. In the next round of trials, I plan to ground both man and dog (in that order) while exposing them to a low-intensity electrical field. That may shed more light on the exact cause of this complicated phobia by simulating more closely the actual events occurring during electrical storms.

If the primary cause of thunderstorm phobia is that dogs are receiving small static shocks during storms, it would explain why programs focused on desensitizing dogs to the sound of thunder meet with little success. It would also explain why treatment with anxiety-reducing drugs is only partially effective and why conductive surfaces and bathroom appliances are so popular with thunderstorm-phobic dogs during a storm. Presumably, affected dogs learn about these safe places by trial and error, much as rats do in a classical conditioned-avoidance test. In this test, the experimenter arranges for small electric shocks to be delivered through the metal floor of the cage, but the rats have a safe place in their cage, usually a pedestal or shelf, where they do not receive the shocks. The rat quickly learns which part of the cage is safe.

In support of the electrical theory of thunderstorm phobia, I have had two owners to date report to me that they get shocks from their dogs when they touch them during a storm. In addition, longhorn cattle in Texas are sometimes seen to have a greenish electrical discharge flickering from the tips of their horns during a storm. This phenomenon of static leak through the sharp points of the cattle's horns is known as St. Elmo's fire. (It can also be seen from the tips of the masts of sailing ships and around the windows and along the wing tips of modern airplanes during electric storms.) The point of the cattle story is that at least one other species is known to become charged with static electricity during storms.

I became quite confident about my electrical theory and was looking for any exception that might disprove the rule. It was with great interest, then, that I read in Elizabeth Marshall Thomas's book *The Hidden Life of Dogs* that one of her Huskies had pressed itself behind the pipes in the bathroom when her Cambridge apartment had been burglarized. Ms. Marshall Thomas attributed the dog's fear to the burglary and assumed that the dog was seeking a small, denlike place in which to hide. Needless to say, I was obliged to call her and ask whether her dog was known to be thunderstorm-phobic. She pondered the question for a short while and then replied enthusiastically, "Why, yes, he was. Now I remember—he was extremely storm-phobic." I breathed a sigh of relief.

The most logical approach to treating thunderstorm phobia is to combine a desensitization program with a strategy for preventing the buildup of static electricity. This is what I intend to do in future clinical cases. At some time in the future, I'll be able to compare treatment with and without electrical grounding. Until then, a theory is only a theory, but I think this is a good one: it explains what we see.

Thunderstorm Phobia

This manifests itself as a fearful response during storms (seeking owner's presence, panting, pacing, salivating). Afflicted dogs are often frightened of isolated components of storms (such as thunder itself, darkening skies, wind noise, rain, etc.) and thunder facsimiles (sonic booms, blasting, cars backfiring, etc.).

Treatment

1. Systematic desensitization and counterconditioning to sound recordings of thunder may be palliative in mildly affected dogs and should be part of any retraining program, but this approach is unlikely to be effective on its own for moderately or severely affected individuals.
2. Measures to prevent static electrical charge buildup may have preventive value and might be helpful as part of a desensitization program.
3. Antianxiety medication, such as buspirone, is extremely helpful, particularly in severely affected dogs.

CHAPTER 8

Will You Still Need Me, Will You Still Feed Me . . . ?

Most of the behavior problems I see at our clinic are in dogs under three years old. Some of the problems are simply management ones. This is especially true in the case of young puppies, which, inebriated with their own joie de vivre, almost literally run circles around their unsuspecting owners, jumping up, barking, chewing, and doing all the other things that puppies do—and not always when and where they should. A slightly more insidious group of behavior problems presents itself in juvenile, adolescent, and young adult dogs, between six months and three years. This latter group of problems relates mainly to aggression toward owners, fear of people (with or without aggression), and in some cases to situational fears such as separation anxiety. Between three and nine years, most of these behavior problems appear less frequently and in a most desultory way (with the possible exception of thunderstorm phobia, which seems to get worse suddenly in the middle of this period). When dogs reach the age of nine or ten years, most owners have come to accept them for what they are and have learned to live with their idiosyncracies or work around them. New behavior problems can and do surface in this geriatric group; when they do, such problems are often linked to the gradual consequences of aging. There is one geriatric syndrome that I have become particularly interested in, which I refer to as geriatric (or late-onset) separation anxiety. This is a fascinating syndrome with multiple causes that most often presents itself as nocturnal distress. Fortunately, most affected dogs can be treated quite successfully and made to feel much more comfortable.

A typical history associated with geriatric separation anxiety is for an older dog suddenly to start showing intense anxiety, particularly at night, keeping its owners awake by pacing, panting, and pawing at them, constantly demanding attention. Curiously, affected dogs are often relatively normal during the day, though some may show anxiety bouts even during daylight hours if they become physically separated from their owners (classical separation anxiety). Dogs with geriatric separation anxiety appear to view their owner's sleep as a form of separation, and the consequences are very similar to those observed in other fear-based conditions, such as thunderstorm phobia. Most affected dogs have been mildly nervous or anxious throughout their lives, perhaps suffering from borderline separation anxiety, but never really developing the full-blown syndrome. Why, then, should this problem suddenly worsen in old age?

I saw my first case of this condition through a referral by our own internal medicine service at Tufts. Our internists had been consulted by the owner of an aging Afghan that showed increasing nocturnal anxiety, involving a good deal of vocalization, panting, pacing, and attention-getting behavior. The veterinary specialists examined the dog repeatedly and ran all kinds of sophisticated blood tests, but they drew a complete blank regarding any medical diagnosis. I was consulted as an afterthought, more as a pharmacologist than as a behaviorist, to prescribe some palliative medication for these symptoms. The idea was to ease the poor dog's distress and permit the dog and its owners to get some rest. I did as I was bid and prescribed a mild anxiety-reducing medication, buspirone, which worked rather well. The dog was much more peaceful at night and even seemed more relaxed during the day. Everyone was sleeping once again, and even the owner's anxiety level plummeted. However, I knew something had to be underlying the behavioral signs. About 2 weeks later the dog broke a bone in its leg while walking down some steps. The fracture was sudden, spontaneous, and seemingly inexplicable. The dog was rushed to the hospital, where it received an orthopedic examination, including X-rays and a bone scan. The dog had sustained what is termed a pathological fracture, a fracture resulting from bone disease—in this case, a bone tumor. The dog then went on to chemotherapy and was no longer under my care, but this case started me thinking about the possible behavioral consequences of undiagnosed disease. I figured that the dog knew what was going on before we did and was acting anxiously because it was experiencing discomfort. This discomfort, I reasoned, would make the dog insecure and more needy of attention. After all, kids never like to be left alone when they are ill, and even adults need extra nurturing when confronted with an overwhelming medical problem. No one likes to go it alone.

The next dog I saw with late-onset separation anxiety turned out to have a brain tumor. Following that there was a dog with severe arthritis, a dog with a chronic slipped disk problem, and then a German Shepherd with a neurological condition, which caused it to lose the use of its hind legs. The medical causes were diverse, but the behavioral syndrome was quite consistent.

I was beginning to gain confidence in my ability to diagnose this syndrome when I was presented with my next case of late-onset separation anxiety. Dolly, a twelve-year-old liver-and-white English Springer Spaniel, was brought to me by her co-owners, Theresa Flowers and Elizabeth Denver. Dolly had a six-month history of what her owners called "panic attacks." I immediately felt at ease with these owners, as they were both relaxed, organized, articulate, and extremely logical. I never did find out much about them, but their matter-of-fact, though concerned, attitude helped the consultation run smoothly and efficiently. I thought that they must have been schoolteachers. Dolly gave a good display of the behavior she was credited with as she whined and paced her way around the consulting room, looking extremely anxious at times. Elizabeth lead off the dialogue.

"I can't figure out what's up with Dolly," she said. "I wrote down on your sheet that she's having panic attacks. I don't even know if dogs get panic attacks, but that's certainly what it looks like to me. She gets some sleep at night in the kitchen, on a sofa, or in her bed, but, recently, as soon as she wakes up—very early in the morning, before it's even light outside—she begins to bark. We have a see-through fireplace in the wall and she stands there looking through the glass, whining, yapping, and crying, waiting for someone to come. Sometimes she gets so worked up she even vomits up bile. When we finally come down to calm her, she greets us enthusiastically. Basically, she's all over us, and the panic subsides for a while. She has some attacks during the day as well. She has started following us around and cries and barks if we end up separated in different places inside the house. She also cries and barks if she is not allowed to follow us outside. If she does come out, she sticks pretty close to us. If we have to leave her during the week, she barks all day, and when we come back, she starts barking and jumping at the kitchen windows and nearly knocks us down when we come in. In the evening, she rests close to us while we read or watch TV, but cries and whines if anyone leaves the room, and sometimes starts pacing around. She seems to be particularly attached to me, because if I go outside to take one of the other dogs out at night, she barks and jumps at the window until I come back in. As flattering as this behavior is, it really is a problem for us, and I think she feels bad. What is going on, Dr. Dodman? Do you have any idea?"

"If it started suddenly six months ago, and there was no indication of any behavior like this before, I would be very suspicious that there's a medical condition contributing to some underlying anxiety problem," I said. "Have you had her thoroughly checked over?"

"Yes," said Theresa. "We took her to a vet, who referred us to a specialist. Both examined her and found nothing. She had various blood tests and at one point was put on a course of antihistamines. That did no good at all. Somebody advised us to change her diet from a performance ration to low-protein food. We did that and it had no effect either, so we're at a loss."

"Even though you've had her examined thoroughly and came to no conclusion, I feel almost certain that she does have some medical problem," I said. "Maybe it is too early for it to be diagnosed yet—only time will tell." I then proceeded to tell them the stories of the Afghan with the bone tumor and the other dogs with medical conditions that had been brought in with similar problems.

"I thought there might be a medical reason," said Elizabeth, looking at Theresa. "Didn't I say that to you in the car on the way here?"

Theresa nodded.

I examined Dolly but didn't find anything wrong. I didn't need to do blood work because it had already been done, but I asked them to have the results sent for my attention (and for the record) just in case something had been missed.

"Let me give you my behavioral diagnosis," I said. "I'll call this syndrome geriatric separation anxiety. Pending review of Dolly's medical records and blood work, I would like to suggest the following treatment. First, you should cautiously step up her exercise to help burn off some of her nervous energy. I would also suggest that you continue with the all-natural low-protein diet, as this is at least a step in the right direction. Then I would suggest that you start building up her confidence by giving her a job to do. Even something as simple as training her to go to her bed and stay, or teaching her 'Wait,' would be helpful exercises. In general, she should be encouraged to be more independent. Don't punish her, but give her plenty of praise, petting, and food rewards if she does what you want her to do. In other words, give her direction and rewards, not correction. In the meantime, let's try a short course of buffered aspirin and an anxiety-reducing medication to make her feel a bit more comfortable. I'd like you to check back with me every couple of weeks."

The pair nodded their approval of this plan, I shook hands with them, and we parted amicably. Over the next few weeks, I had several phone calls from them and in one of them they asked whether a negative interaction between Dolly and their house-keeper could have precipitated the problem. I acknowledged that this was possible but directed them back to our original medical hypothesis. Apparently the aspirin alone had not helped a great deal, but Dolly was becoming a little calmer as the antianxiety medication took effect. Then one day a few weeks later, my secretary, Karen, rushed up to me with an excited look on her face, obviously bursting with some hot news.

"Dr. Dodman," she said, "Elizabeth Denver just called. Her dog developed a swelling above her left eye and was rushed to an ophthalmologist for attention. He diagnosed a tumor behind Dolly's eye and operated on it immediately. That was a few days ago, and since then Dolly has been fine. No separation anxiety at all. She's as good as new!" I must admit, I was quite chuffed about this new turn of events.

My most recent case of late-onset separation anxiety was in an extremely mild-mannered mixed-breed dog called Sympathy. Sympathy was owned by a contractor named Jonathan Knapik, who clearly had a lot of emotional investment in his dog. Jonathan had rescued Sympathy from an abusive situation when the dog was one year old, and although he was aware that Sympathy was a little on the nervous side, preferring to stay close to him at all times, no real problem had emerged until one fateful day. Jonathan, whose home was in suburban Boston, was upstairs shaving one morning while Sympathy waited patiently in the car in the street below. Jonathan had rolled the car window down ten inches or so, so that Sympathy could stick her head out and look around. All was peaceful. Just then, Jonathan heard police sirens and the sound of people running and shouting in the street. He looked out of the window to see what was going on and saw a man run past the house, hotly pursued by one of Boston's finest. At this point, Sympathy leaped out of the car window and started to chase the police officer down the street. The officer stopped after a few feet, turned around, and kicked the dog, which then proceeded to grab the officer by the trouser cuff. As all of this was going on Jonathan rushed downstairs and approached the now battling duo. He yelled to the officer that Sympathy was his dog and that things would be fine if he could grab her. As he bent down to get hold of Sympathy by the collar, the officer took out his .38 caliber revolver and shot the dog in the side of the head. Sympathy collapsed to the ground and the police officer continued his pursuit, leaving Jonathan kneeling beside what he thought was a dying dog. Jonathan rushed Sympathy to his vet's office, where the bleeding was stemmed. To Jonathan's delight, Sympathy recovered, although she was deaf in one ear because the bullet had damaged her auditory nerve. Apparently the slug had passed into the skull just in front of Sympathy's ear, traveled through the various auditory structures and down through the neck, and come to rest in Sympathy's chest wall. In a way, the dog was lucky; her fate could have been a lot worse. As it turns out, the physical complications of her injuries were not as bad as the repercussions of the psychological trauma, as Jonathan was about to find out.

From that day on, Sympathy was petrified of police cars, vehicles that looked like police cars, flashing lights, and, of course, police officers. Also, she could no longer stand to be separated from Jonathan by either distance or sleep. The distance component wasn't a problem, because Jonathan always took Sympathy everywhere with him. He loved that dog, and there is no doubt that Sympathy lived solely for him. At work, Jonathan would stand on the construction site and know that Sympathy was somewhere in the undergrowth peering out. Sympathy never took her eyes off Jonathan. Jonathan would make a simple hand signal at any time during the day and Sympathy would come running to him. She was never caught unawares. None of this was really a problem for Sympathy or Jonathan . . . until nighttime. Every night when Jonathan turned in, Sympathy started whining, pacing, whimpering, and pawing at the bed. When I first saw Jonathan, this had been going on for a year and a half, and Jonathan was getting about as much sleep as the mother of a newborn baby. Jonathan's twenty-five-year-old son was with him in the consulting room, and at the end of their story, they both leaned forward and looked at me very intensely.

"You've got to help us," they said almost in unison, and I knew they were serious. "We could never have her put down, but we just can't go on like this," Jonathan added.

Jonathan seemed to be extremely on edge, probably as a result of sleep deprivation. He was between a rock and hard place. Sympathy's case was not quite as simple as some of the other geriatric separation anxiety cases I had seen; there were both physical and primary psychological causes of the anxiety, and I wasn't sure which was having the most impact. The psychological effects struck me as similar to post-traumatic stress syndrome, well known to war veterans. With this in mind, I gave Jonathan all the usual supportive information that I provide to the owners of dogs with uncomplicated separation anxiety, but I also talked to him about medication as a mainstay of treatment. I knew that Jonathan and his son were desperate for a speedy resolution to the nighttime problem, and I also felt that Sympathy was suffering psychological and perhaps physical pain. Fortunately, the drug amitriptyline covers both bases, treating anxiety as well as providing analgesia. Although an antidepressant, amitriptyline is sometimes used to treat chronic pain in humans. With the combination of behavioral modi-fication, designed to instill confidence in Sympathy, and medica-tion, I thought that the dog's chances for a significant improvement were good.

Amitriptyline usually takes several days to kick in, and Sympa-thy's case was no exception. During this period I had a phone call from a concerned Jonathan, who was still not getting his fair share of sleep. Eventually, however, after a week or two, he called back with the joyous news that Sympathy had slept right through the night.

"This medication is amazing," he said. "I haven't seen Sympathy like this for years. I tell you, she's a new dog. Talk about bright-eyed and bushy-tailed! How can I ever thank you?"

Well, he didn't need to thank me. The good news was reward enough in itself. Needless to say, I advised him to continue the behavior-modification therapy to ensure sustained improvement, but because I suspected that physical pain was a factor, I had a feeling that it would never be possible to wean Sympathy off the medication entirely. I saw Sympathy several times over the next few months, and for the most part her improvement was maintained. There were a few minor setbacks that I dealt with by using Valium as a supplementary treatment, and more recently I have had to fortify the analgesic component with an opioid, butorphanol. De-spite these wobbles, Sympathy is considerably better than she ever was, and Jonathan and his son are getting some well-deserved rest. I believe that Sympathy was extremely lucky to have an owner as dedicated as Jonathan. There are many people who would have given up a lot earlier, but in this case persistence paid off.

Geriatric (or late-onset) separation anxiety is not the only behav-ioral condition that affects older dogs. There is a whole spectrum of physical and mental deterioration that can contribute to altered behavior in older dogs. The mental degenerative changes have recently been dubbed cognitive dysfunction syndrome, or canine Alzheimer's disease. Signs of this latter condition range from dullness and lethargy to elimination disorders. Fortunately, a new medical treatment for this syndrome is being explored by one of the drug companies, and the early results look extremely promising. Before too long, it should be possible to prolong a quality existence for dogs like Sympathy and those affected with canine Alzheimer's by a combination of behavioral and environmental management and appropriate pharmacological treatment. It is becoming apparent that it's not enough to simply need and feed our old friends; we have to make sure they are comfortable as well.

• TREATMENT FOR •

Geriatric (Late-Onset) Separation Anxiety

This condition presents itself as a sudden exacerbation of otherwise mild separation anxiety later in life. Many affected dogs become anxious at night when their owners attempt to sleep. Symptoms include attention seeking, pacing, whining, and sometimes inappropriate elimination of urine or feces.

Treatment

1. A full medical evaluation is called for, including a complete blood count, blood-chemistry profile, and urinalysis. X-rays and other tests should be ordered where indicated.

2. Medical treatment as indicated. Medication can be prescribed to relieve anxiety or pain. Anxiety-reducing drugs include buspirone and Valium-type drugs or antidepressants. Analgesics such as aspirin and opioids such as butorphanol may be needed, and anti-inflammatory drugs, such as cortisone, can also be helpful in some cases. (Note: Do not give aspirin to a dog or cat without veterinary approval.)

3. Supportive psychologic therapy, including independence training (see "The dog who loved too much"), may also be indicated to reinstill confidence in the dog once medical matters have been addressed.

4. Plenty of exercise (physical factors permitting), a sensible diet, and daily obedience training (using positive reinforcement techniques) are helpful background measures.

CHAPTER 9

A Shot in the Dark

I t was a warm July morning, and the sunshine was filtering through the trees in front of the Foster Hospital for Small Animals. During a brief respite between cases, I was taking a little time to absorb the natural beauty of our hospital's setting. The dean often describes our school, nestling in its 640-acre central New England campus, as the "dandiest little veterinary school in the country." The campus was formerly a state mental hospital that, along with many other such hospitals nationally, was emptied in large part because of the discovery of revolutionary drug therapies for schizophrenia and other psychiatric conditions. It's ironic that such pharmacological treatments resulted in the conversion of many state hospitals for other uses, paving the way for our school, our behavior program, and, stemming from the behavior program, novel pharmacological treatments for animal behavior problems.

My thoughts were interrupted by someone paging me from the reception desk. "Dr. Dodman, your next client has arrived," said the voice.

I turned to see a slightly built, well-dressed woman, Debra Reed, standing by the desk with a German Shepherd in tow. Our eyes met, and I walked toward her to greet her. So as not to incite her dog, I avoided looking at the animal directly, looking instead at Debra and viewing the dog with my now well-developed peripheral vision. The dog, Lady, a sixty-pound, four-year-old German Shepherd, surveyed me with interest and ran a quick sensory scan. Apparently everything met with her approval, and she remained at ease. Debra and I entered the consulting room, exchanging pleasantries. I continued to survey Lady for any clues as to the problem she'd been brought in for, but there were none. At this stage, I had to assess her as a fairly well adjusted dog. I did notice, however, that she tended to stay quite close to her owner and may have been a tad shy: typical German Shepherd behavior.

I learned that Debra had acquired Lady from a friend in Maine when Lady was approximately twelve to eighteen months old. Lady had not been too impressed by her new home at first and had lain around all day, displaying little in the way of personality. Debra described her as "acting like a geriatric." In retrospect, Lady may have been depressed following her relocation, as these signs, coupled with a reduced appetite and sleep disturbances, are typical of depression. In any event, the depression lifted as Lady responded to the kindness she was shown by the Reeds. Because of Lady's mild shyness and her checkered history of ownership, I began to suspect some anxiety or fear-based condition. Debra's next comments confirmed my hunch.

"The problem," she said, "is that although Lady is a wonderful pet, she has this really odd reaction every time I go near the windows, especially if I touch the microblinds. She may be just resting quietly, minding her own business, but when she sees me moving toward the window, she jumps up and looks apprehensive. If I continue to approach the window, she starts to pace and whine, and if I actually touch the plastic rod that operates the blind, she loses control completely. Even if I leave the room at this point, it takes an hour or more for her to settle down."

This was indeed a most unusual problem. Although Lady's behavior was a classic phobic response, I couldn't understand why Lady would become so agitated when her owner went to touch the blind.

"When did this start?" I asked, thinking that the answer to that question might provide some clues.

"Shortly after we got her. It seems that she has always been scared of our touching the blinds, although she has become steadily worse with time. It's a real problem for us now, because we live in a ground-floor apartment; for privacy I have to shut the blinds at night, and I need to open them again in the morning to let the daylight in."

"She does this every time you go to the blind?" I asked.

"Every single time, without fail. We just don't know what to do. Someone we spoke to said that we should employ the 'happy routine,' acting happy before we open the blinds. All that did was make her frightened earlier because she knew what was coming next. At one time we thought that maybe it was the sound the blinds make that was causing her a problem, so we tried playing loud music. We had no luck with that either. Our vet told us to try a technique called flooding, in which we twiddled with the blind constantly, ignoring her reaction until it subsided. We tried that too, but she just didn't settle down at all, even after we twiddled for what seemed like hours. If anything, she seemed to be getting worse the longer we stayed there."

I decided to try to home in on possible causes.

"Do you think that she could have been scared or hurt at one time while the blind was being operated?" I asked, fishing for a clue. "I mean some years ago, when the problem first started?"

"The only really bad thing that ever happened to her," said Debra, "was right after we got her, when our neighbor shot her with his air gun because she got into his vegetable garden. That upset her a lot. I had just let her out for her evening walk, and she must have jumped the fence. The next thing I heard was a *phhht*, followed by a yelp, and Lady came running back with her tail between her legs. We reported the man for cruelty, but there was nothing else we could do. We don't speak to each other these days."

"So where was this man when he shot her?" I asked.

"He was inside his house," said Debra.

"I see. So he must have shot through the window," I said. "Does he have microblinds, too?"

She nodded. The light was beginning to dawn for both of us.

"That would do it," I said. "If Lady heard a microblind being raised and then experienced sharp pain, she might associate the two events. That would explain everything that we see here. She was at a suitably impressionable age, and the primary stimulus— the pain—was intense enough to produce a profound and lasting memory of the event. The sound of the microblind simply became coupled with this extremely unpleasant experience. We see the same type of thing in dogs that have had a bad experience at the vet's office—say, a painful injection. These dogs may be frightened of getting into the car, people with white coats, or the smell of rubbing alcohol because these stimuli have become coupled with the unpleasant event itself."

"Do fears usually get worse like this?" Debra asked. "After all, it's been a long time since she was shot. Why should she continue to harbor the association?"

"Good question," I said. "This pattern of development is common for many fears and phobias. They usually start at mild to moderate intensity and then escalate to extreme proportions. I believe that the fearful response itself is so unpleasant that it is self-reinforcing, causing the problem to worsen. For example, let's say a person has a fear of public speaking, and every time they speak their heart beats twice as fast, they have butterflies in their stomach, and their hands sweat and shake. Such a person might become queasy at even the thought of speaking or at the sight of a lectern. The whole experience is so debilitating that fear turns into dread."

"That makes sense. So how are we going to treat it?" asked Debra.

"We'll use a technique called desensitization. The basis of this technique is to introduce a dog very slowly and systematically to something it is afraid of."

I proceeded to outline a desensitization program for Lady in which the microblinds themselves would be the focus of the program. As usual, it was important for me to stress that Lady should not be exposed to the full-intensity stimulus during the retraining process, which meant that Debra had to decide whether the blinds should stay permanently up or permanently down.

I saw her face fall as she contemplated the choice between a lack of privacy or an absence of daylight. It took a little more encouragement before I managed to persuade her to bite the bullet, so to speak, but in the end she decided that the blinds would stay down.

I walked Debra through the specific steps of the desensitization program, starting with teaching her how to make Lady sit and stay in return for a delicious food reward. This sit-stay operation was to be conducted first at a distance from the blinds—for example, in the yard or in the hallway—and then moved progressively nearer to the offending blinds as the dog successfully completed the sit-stay exercises at the more remote locations. Of course, at a later stage I intended to have Debra touch and then operate the blinds, but only when Lady's responses to the earlier exercises showed that she was ready. I discussed with Debra the option of prescribing an anxiety-reducing medication, specifically buspirone. She elected to have Lady medicated in this way to facilitate the behavior-modification program and to expedite her full recovery. Debra and Lady left the clinic, leaving me to my next case. I jotted down a few supplementary notes and then continued with the rest of my day.

I didn't speak to Debra again for two weeks. In a telephone consultation, she informed me that the sit-stay program was working well and that Lady was now able to sit for several minutes right underneath the window without showing any signs of fear or anxiety. I was pleased with this report and suggested that she might advance to the next stage, that of actually moving to touch the microblind. I didn't think it was wise for her to grab the control rod suddenly and twiddle it right away, so I advised her to split up the action into its component parts. She would start, for example, by raising her hand in the direction of the blind, progressing a few inches closer each session until she was able to touch the control rod without causing the fearful response. Debra agreed this was a reasonable next step, so we left it there for the time being. We spoke a couple of weeks after that, at the one-month follow-up. Lady was doing even better. Debra had advanced with the program to the point where she was raising and lowering the microblind while Lady remained in the sitting position. When released, Lady would return to her basket in the corner of the room. Although she wasn't exactly in the mood for play after her exercises, at least the puffing, panting, and hysteria were gone. I advised Debra to wean Lady off the medication, as I believed that it had now done its job. Naturally, I asked her to continue the behavior-modification therapy throughout the weaning period and at weekly intervals thereafter. Debra was delighted with Lady's progress (which was subsequently maintained) and even volunteered additional testimony about the "miraculous cure." Apparently Lady had been so frightened of her microblind-containing environment that she had to be carried back into the house after the Reeds had been away for the weekend. Now they only had to pick up her bed, and she would walk in herself. Talk about the Lazarus cure.

A few weeks later, I found myself dealing with another unusual phobic dog. The dog was an eight-year-old sable-and-white Collie. The owner, Keith Davis, caught me a little off guard when he announced at the beginning of the behavioral interview that his dog was phobic of Thursdays. He said this with a smile on his face, so I knew there was more to come—or at least I hoped there was, because I didn't think that dogs had any idea of the day of the week. I glanced at the dog, Tammy, which, unlike Lady, was not at all composed in the consulting room. Tammy was obviously anxious —panting, salivating, and constantly pulling on her lead. There was no doubt about her underlying personality. Even without the introductory remarks, I would have anticipated some kind of fearful behavior. Keith proceeded to explain that Thursday was trash collection day and that Tammy became scared the minute they started to bag the trash, even if they did this the night before. On the morning of the trash collection, Tammy would take up a position at the top of the stairs and stare down anxiously as Keith and his wife put the trash bags outside the door at around seven o'clock. The dog's fear would mount as the day progressed, until eventually Tammy became hysterical, running back and forth and up and down the stairs, panting, whining, salivating, and generally whipping herself into a frenzy. Her owners would usually apprehend her early in one of these outbursts and confine her to the cellar, where she continued to panic, but down there Tammy's reaction didn't seem quite as bad. Of late, Keith had been confining Tammy to the cellar from the beginning of the day on Thursdays, only to take her out on their return from work in the late afternoon. They would usually find the floor covered with saliva, and Tammy would appear still mildly agitated. It turned out that Tammy had some other fears as well. She was afraid of wind noise and the sound of shutters banging against the side of the house. She was also afraid of sudden, loud noises, such as sneezing or a pager beeping, and would start pacing back and forth, unable to rest after such events. The worst fear of all was the sight or sound of the garbage truck.

Apparently Tammy's phobia had started about a year before. Before that time, she had always been let out of the house at seven in the morning to run around and take care of business. This never caused her any problem initially, even on Thursdays. Prior to the development of her phobia, the garbage truck didn't arrive until around eleven A.M., by which time she was usually in the house, sleeping peacefully, waiting for her owners to return. One Thursday, however, almost exactly one year previously, the truck was rerouted, arriving at the Davises' house at 7:15. That day Tammy had been let out as usual and was nosing around outside. All of a sudden, she ran back into the house, terrified, her legs a blur beneath her as she scrambled up the stairs and went into hiding. Her owners knew that something terrible must have happened. Given her propensity for sound phobias, it seems likely that the medley of the beeping sounds made by the garbage truck, the banging and scraping sounds of the compactor, the noise of air escaping from the compressor, the clanking of trash cans, and men shouting must have been nightmarish cacophony for her. This was the embodiment of her worst dreams. Whatever happened, it had changed her forever, or so it seemed. Was there anything we could do to make life a little bit more tolerable for this poor dog? After all, there's a Thursday every week.

Keith told me the things he had tried so far. He had tried tying her to the support columns in the cellar to prevent her from walking around. The result was that she salivated profusely and evacuated her bowels out of sheer terror. He had also tried confining her in a small area behind a wooden gate, but she had become hysterical and made matchwood out of the gate. Playing the radio to drown out the sound of the garbage truck had not worked either. Even his attempts to distract her at critical times with a tennis ball (her favorite toy) were unsuccessful. Keith had even been to see his local vet and had tried some medications (probably progesterone-like hormone treatments) that made Tammy drink like a fish but didn't solve the problem.

Keith and Tammy had certainly run the gamut of home treatments. It is always good to know what hasn't worked because then you don't have to try it again. In behavior-modification therapy, there is a simple rule of thumb that if something doesn't begin to work within three to five days, then it probably won't work at all and it's time to change tactics. (Treatment with antidepressants is an exception to this general rule, as they may take three to six weeks to show an effect.) One of the things Keith was doing— attempting to distract the dog with the tennis ball—was a step in the right direction, but he needed a little help with the program. As with Lady, my recommendation was to have Tammy treated by means of a desensitization program with simultaneous counterconditioning using food treats or a tennis ball as a reward. Keith was also advised to find the garbage truck depot and to take Tammy as close to the trucks as she would permit without showing signs of nervousness. He was to play with her and give her food treats for ten minutes or so, and then take her back home. During subsequent sessions, he was to attempt to get progressively closer until eventually he could take her right up to the truck and play with her without her showing any signs of anxiety. I advised him to be patient and content himself with a gradual improvement. The next stage, with the cooperation of the driver, would be to repeat the procedure with the vehicle's engine running and then gradually to phase in various components of the sound of the truck in operation until Tammy was comfortable with the whole experience. Last, and most important, I gave instructions that Tammy should not be exposed to the full brunt of the garbage truck experience during the retraining program. I wasn't sure how Keith was going to manage this, but he decided to ask the municipal workers to stop the truck a couple of houses down the road, at least for a few weeks. To my surprise, they agreed, and the program was initiated.

Keith phoned me four days later, in a panic himself. He said the program just wasn't working. He had driven Tammy right up to a garbage truck at the city dump and had taken her out of the car, whereupon she immediately developed a full-blown phobic attack and had to be bundled back into the car quickly and driven off. I reexplained the importance of the gradual introduction to him—he had somehow failed to grasp this—and he went off to try again. A few phone calls later, it became apparent that for some reason Keith seemed to have a mental block regarding desensitization, as he just kept driving right up to the truck and terrifying the dog. He even invented his own embellishments, which fell more into the category of flooding. Fat chance, I thought.

Eventually, I tried another tack and had him make a tape recording of the sounds made by the garbage truck. I asked him to work with Tammy at home, exposing her to the sounds first at a low level, then gradually increasing the volume, and rewarding her (with warm praise, food treats, and the tennis ball) for remaining calm and following directions. He excelled at this task and came home for lunch every day to work with Tammy. He called me back some six months after the original appointment to say that he was now able to turn up the sound so high that it seemed like the garbage truck was in the room . . . and Tammy remained calm. As Keith had progressed through the desensitization program, he had decided to introduce Tammy to the trash collectors, who had good-heartedly agreed to come in now and then to say some kind words, feed her treats, and pet her. These strategies together had worked so well that Tammy overcame her fear of Thursdays entirely after about six months of therapy. She still disliked wind noise, banging shutters, and the rest, and we could have worked on these other phobias one by one, but Keith was happy with what he'd accomplished and decided to end the consultations.

Sights and sounds are not the only stimuli to which dogs can develop phobias. Some even become terrified by apparently innocuous stimuli such as smells. I always imagine that dogs that are phobic about odors must be relating the smell to some other previously associated unpleasant event, because it is hard to see how most odors (barring things like smelling salts) could be aversive per se. This may have been the case with one phobic dog a colleague of mine saw, which was frightened by the smell of lamb cooking. No doubt the odor itself caused the dog no harm, and one can only surmise what may have happened to the poor creature one day when roast lamb was on the menu. Memories can be recalled or enhanced by odors, even for us humans, with our relatively inferior olfactory sense. Even we can be transported back in time when we encounter a particular odor, whether it's the musty smell of an old church or a particular brand of cologne. Yet the sensory epithelium of our noses only occupies an area about the size of a human thumbnail, whereas the dog's olfactory epithelium is closer in size to the area occupied by an unfolded pocket handkerchief. That's nothing to sniff at!

It seems that whatever the eliciting stimulus for a phobia, the initial aversive event involves pain, discomfort, or some other unpleasant sensation. Any incidental stimulus associated with the event may then become indelibly linked with the unpleasant or painful experience; each time the animal encounters that stimulus later, it anticipates more of the same grief. By a learning process termed backchaining, the linked stimulus may then itself become associated with some other event or circumstance, so that truly innocuous things can become initiating stimuli for a phobic reaction, such as the microblinds for Lady and the trash bags for Tammy. One dog I saw recently had a summer phobia—more specifically, a phobia related to flying insects, the very presence of which would trigger full-blown attacks. On careful questioning of this dog's owner, I learned that when still a puppy, the dog had been shut in a car with a dozen or so horseflies. The flies had savagely bitten the poor creature, leaving a clear and lasting impression of the enemy. The fear subsequently generalized to all flying insects, and the dog then presumably made the connection between flies and summer (and the car). If this can happen with insects, why not people too? Can dogs become phobic of people? I believe they can, and that affected dogs may turn out to be some of the most deeply disturbed and dangerous dogs we know of—but more of that later.

• TREATMENT FOR •

Inanimate Phobias
(Other than Thunderstorm Phobias)

Affected dogs display extreme agitation (panting, pacing, salivating) when exposed to certain sights, sounds, or smells. The cause may not always be obvious, but sometimes a traumatic incident can be identified as having given rise to the underlying fear.

Treatment

1. Identify the source of the fear. A detailed history is important.
2. Start a program of desensitization and counterconditioning. If the instigating cause is long gone (and unlikely to surface again) it is sufficient to desensitize to secondarily associated cues. As usual, patience is a virtue with such programs.
3. Medication (anxiety-reducing drugs, antidepressants) may be prescribed. Beta blockers, such as propranolol (Inderal), can also be helpful.
4. Appropriate attention to exercise (output) and diet (input) may facilitate treatment.

CHAPTER 10

Shy and Sharp

T here are three main fear-inducing stimuli in dogs—living things (such as people or other dogs), inanimate cues (sounds, sights, smells), and various circumstances or situations. I often refer to these as the Bermuda Triangle of fear, from which there is no absolute return. The level of fear generated by a particular stimulus may range from mild anxiety to an intense emotional response activating the fight-or-flight mechanism. The latter is capable of converting an otherwise peaceful dog into a seething maniac. In extreme states of fear, dogs may attack and hurt people, hurtle through tenth-story windows, or wreak havoc in their homes in attempts to escape. Although genetic mechanisms are at work in some fears (a genetically nervous strain of Pointers has been studied for years at the National Institutes of Health), by far the most important initiating factor is environmental experience or conditioning.

Many dogs that are fearful have multiple fears. For example, a dog that's frightened of people may also be frightened of blowing leaves or flapping tarpaulins. The same dog may well suffer from mild separation anxiety or become anxious during visits to the veterinarian's office. When fears are mild, we tend to dismiss them as idiosyncratic. If a fearful dog leaves the room or hides under a settee when visitors arrive, its owners may simply think that the dog is silly for being scared of harmless strangers. If a dog hides when the vacuum cleaner is turned on or looks miserable and whines when left alone, owners may not regard this behavior as a problem. Fear-related conditions are often only recognized when they reach the point where the dog is physically affected or deals with the fear in ways that disturb the owner. A dog that's frightened of thunder may start to pant and pace and cling to its owner. A dog that's frightened of people may growl at them instead of hiding. This is the point when the veterinarian or behaviorist is often consulted.

So what are the environmental influences that cause fear and insecurity to develop in dogs? Probably the same ones that cause them to develop in people: adverse experiences, particularly early in life. Children who have had a disturbed or traumatic childhood and who haven't experienced the benefits of a normal, healthy family environment often develop into dysfunctional adults. Many of these individuals have low self-esteem and either find it difficult to be assertive or turn into control freaks. In dogs that develop fear of people (or other fears), the situation is analogous. Almost all fearful dogs are found to have a canine equivalent of the human dysfunctional background. Many of them are found to have had unfortunate early experiences, including loneliness, uncertainty, and in some cases outright abuse. Sometimes it is possible to document precisely the aversive incidents that occurred early in the dog's life and to chart the intensification and, in some cases, the generalization of the fearful condition. Other times, the cause of the fear is more obscure, and it is a challenge to piece together the known facts to produce a complete picture. One thing is clear—a loving and supportive family and proper socialization are of paramount importance to the normal development of dogs, especially during the first few months of life.

One case really brought home the point about the impact of early aversive events. The dog in question was a Dachshund called Gordy, which belonged to some friends of mine, a veterinarian and his wife. This couple had owned the dog since it was six weeks old, and Gordy had had all the love and attention that his owners could provide. Despite this, it became apparent before too long that Gordy had an extreme dislike of men with white beards. Whenever one would appear, Gordy became hysterical and ran around barking, trying to intimidate the bearded stranger and get rid of him. Initially, it appeared that Gordy had no reason to have developed this fear, as my friends had mollycoddled him for the first six months of his life, treating him more like a baby than a puppy. No aversive events could be recollected, let alone anything connected with men with white beards. Eventually, the problem behavior became so severe that Gordy's owners paid a visit to a nearby animal behaviorist. Under questioning, they recalled that they had left him alone for one day, and therefore did not have firsthand knowledge of his experiences on that day. This had occurred when Gordy was ten and a half weeks old, but on that occasion his owners had a puppy-sitter come to the house to take care of him. The behaviorist's suspicions were aroused by this report.

"The puppy-sitter wasn't a man with a white beard, by any chance?" he asked hopefully.

"No, I'm afraid not," my friend replied. "It was a young woman who works for me."

The behaviorist's spirits sank a little, but then another thought occurred to him.

"Did she have any visitors while you were out?" he ventured.

Neither the veterinarian nor his wife knew the answer to this question, so they had to go back to the source. The young woman in question was located, and she told them that yes, she had indeed had a visitor. It was her boyfriend, and—you guessed it—he had a white beard! She remembered that some kind of shenanigans had occurred during her boyfriend's visit while she was out of the room making tea, but the incident had blown over. My friend's wife then cast her mind back to that evening, and she remembered that when they returned home Gordy had been a little skittish, running around the room, hiding under chairs, and looking fairly anxious. They hadn't been able to figure out why he'd been like that and had just written it off as odd. The next day Gordy had seemed back to normal . . . but he wasn't really. Some negative experience had occurred involving Gordy and the man with the white beard. This experience had been imprinted in the depths of Gordy's mind and was nestling there like a cancer waiting to spread. When men with white beards appeared subsequently, Gordy, who was normally fairly well composed, would suddenly fall to pieces and turn into the hound from hell. As an experiment, the veterinarian managed to persuade the original white-bearded man to visit his clinic while Gordy was there. Mayhem ensued as Gordy exploded into the most aggressive response of his life. Fortunately, he was restrained at the time. This little dog had not allowed his rather specific fear to overwhelm him into cowering, submission, or hiding, but had taken a middle-of-the-road approach, holding his ground and attempting intimidation. Gordy's owners had the option of putting him through a retraining program designed to change his perception of white-bearded men, but instead they preferred the time-honored technique of avoidance. This was an acceptable solution in this case, as Gordy spent most of his life at home and was rarely confronted by strangers, let alone the white-bearded variety.

Some dogs with a similar fear of people are more successful at intimidating and learn quickly how to control a situation, just like their human counterparts. Larger dogs tend to be more successful at this tactic, for obvious reasons. If the dog is both fearful and dominant, there is an extra level of commitment to intimidation, which can then result in serious bites and real danger for the victims of the dog's attacks. These dogs are sometimes referred to by trainers as "shy sharp biters." I have always thought that's a particularly appropriate descriptive term. "Shy sharp" dogs are more dangerous when they have no possibility of escape. When it's fight or flight and there is nowhere to run, that only leaves one alternative. In our hospital, we sometimes come across a fear-aggressive dog that has to be taken out of its cage. If these dogs are approached directly when the cage door is opened, they are likely to become aggressive and may bite. If the person stands to one side to open the door, however, the situation is often completely defused—the dog exits the cage voluntarily and once out is much calmer and safer. Another time that fear-aggressive dogs are more likely to bite is when they are on a short lead or when they're tethered in the yard, two other situations in which escape is not an option. Another important safety tip is that for a dog, the back view of the victim is less threatening than the front, so fearful dogs may bite only as the stranger turns to walk away. Many of these dogs bite on the ankle or back of the thigh. Fearful dogs are least dangerous off the lead and in the open. They may run around a stranger in a wide circle, barking, but in this situation are free to choose how far away they wish to be and to escape if necessary. The result: no aggression.

One of the hallmarks of fear of people is that it is directed toward strangers. These strangers are usually men or children, as it seems it is these two groups that are most likely to treat the dog in an unpleasant and unforgettable way. Men, after all, tend to be more aggressive than women, and we all know the kinds of things that some children do to animals. Boys tend to be worse than girls in this respect, and are therefore more often the targets of canine fear-related aggression. Using retrospective reconstruction, it is sometimes possible to piece together a reasonably accurate guess as to what the original offender looked like. With the veterinarian's dog, it wasn't difficult to guess that the man had a white beard, but other cases are more complex. From what is reported, dogs often fear tall men with hats or beards; big boots and deep voices are also common factors. Sometimes much more subtle cues act as triggers for a fear response, such as the smell of cigarettes or a particular type of perfume. On one occasion, I was consulted regarding a dog that became frightened when anybody who had been drinking appeared in the house, whether they were drunk or not. This report conjured up particularly sad images, but was not a new notion for me, since I have seen a number of dogs that I believe were made dysfunctional by inconsistent interactions with a primary caregiver who was an alcoholic. (Maybe we could learn something about treatment of these dogs from groups such as Adult Children of Alcoholics.)

In some dogs, fear of strangers becomes so generalized that almost any unfamiliar person will elicit some degree of fear response. This makes detective work difficult and full-scale desensitization virtually impossible. The outcome of encounters between strangers and the dog depends to some extent on the reaction of the owners and the stranger. The worst combination is an owner who panics or becomes excited and an apprehensive stranger who nervously tries to make friends with the dog. Family members and people the dog is familiar with do not themselves have any problems with this type of dog, which can be an extremely loving and affectionate family pet. The problems occur only with strangers, and—unlike anxiety-driven territorial aggression, which is much worse at home—fear-related aggression of this magnitude is fairly consistent from place to place.

One patient of mine, called Charlie, a middle-sized black and tan mixed-breed dog who looked part Labrador, part German Shepherd, and part Pit Bull, presented a rather extreme version of fear of people. His fear manifested itself as aggressive, violent lunging and biting attacks directed at all strangers. His was one of the most severe cases of fear-related aggression I have ever seen. He was so bad that I was obligated to discuss with the owners the potentially serious consequences of owning such a dog, but, luckily for Charlie, his owners were resolute that Charlie was here to stay. A trainer friend describes this type of animal as Charles Manson in a dog suit. Quite an accurate description in this case, I thought—even the name was right. Although Charlie was dangerous, I felt sorry for him because I knew that it was some extreme adverse circumstances or experiences that had made him this way. His owners,

Jessie and John McDonald, brought him into the consulting room through the side entrance to avoid any possibility of his attacking the clients in the waiting room.

Jessie was obviously extremely devoted to Charlie. John was not quite so attached, and I gathered he was just there for moral support. There we were in the consulting room, the three of us—and Charlie. Within the first few minutes of the interview, I became very conscious that Charlie, who was rumbling a low growl at me and pulling back his lips slightly, had his eyes firmly fixed on my feet. The desk I was sitting at was a sort of partners desk, and my feet, shuffle as they would, were positioned in the tunnel under the desk. Charlie made for the desk several times during the conversation and, growling, disappeared from view, with Jessie tugging weakly at his lead. I tried to stay calm as I slowly moved my feet back as far as they would possibly go and instructed her firmly to pull Charlie back into my field of vision. Charlie was approximately nineteen months old and, true to form, had been acquired from a pound when he was four or five months old. He had been neutered when he was nine months old, but neutering does nothing for fearful conditions. During the interview, it emerged that the Mc-Donalds had been to see another behaviorist, who diagnosed play aggression and put Charlie on some kind of medication. I don't know how old Charlie was at the time of that consultation, but what I was looking at was not play aggression—and, anyway, why would anyone treat play anything with medication? Even Charlie's owners acknowledged that he had a severe behavior problem and that he was basically out of control. At home he displayed willfulness and dominance, but wasn't a mortal threat to the McDonalds. If dominance had been the only problem, he would never have been a threat to me in the consulting room. As the interview progressed I learned how Charlie would bark and jump at visitors to their house, sometimes snapping at them or biting them. The McDonalds had become recluses . . . but not by choice. None of their friends would visit them anymore. Charlie "wasn't too well behaved" in veterinary offices either. I could see that for myself, and I grew progressively more tense as the details of a few rather nasty incidents were explained to me. I sat there watching Charlie pacing around, blowing hard, intermittently growling and glancing maliciously at my feet. I began to conclude that somebody must have kicked him when he was young for him to have developed a foot fetish of this magnitude.

Treatment advice was what the McDonalds sought, and treatment advice was what I had to provide. I went through my usual repertoire of discussing changes in diet and exercise, informing the McDonalds that a low-protein diet might be beneficial and suggesting that they avoid foods containing artificial preservatives. The McDonalds then told me that Charlie had a known allergic reaction to the food preservative ethoxyquin, so that was something to avoid like the plague. As far as exercise was concerned, I told the McDonalds that the more exercise he got, the better it would be for him (and for all of us), but clearly there were some limiting factors in trying to provide exercise for a dog such as Charlie. I personally wouldn't have wanted to stumble across him in the local park! Obedience training was stressed in order to try to help the McDonalds get better control of Charlie. They were advised to practice the time-honored technique of issuing one-word commands and rewarding the desired response—positive reinforcement. Luckily, they both had a good working knowledge of training techniques, but somehow they had failed to appreciate the importance of conducting daily training sessions to keep Charlie's response consistent. Also, they didn't realize that they were supposed to be aiming for a 100 percent response, at least in optimal circumstances, such as the peace and quiet of their own home. If a dog responds only 70 percent of the time under ideal circumstances, his owners won't have a prayer when there are distractions around. Exercise, a modified diet, and obedience training would probably improve Charlie's disposition, but we were going to need more than that to make him safe.

For the next stage of his treatment, I decided to explain the concept of desensitization, in which Charlie would be gradually exposed to a few of the McDonalds' friends. First, the least threatening of these individuals would be presented at a safe distance, and Charlie would be required to sit calmly, being rewarded for his composure with food treats. Providing treats (or some other pleasant experience), I reasoned, should cause Charlie to associate the previously threatening experience with a pleasurable response rather than fear. On subsequent trials, the volunteer would be asked to approach Charlie slowly as long as he remained under control and appreciative of the treats. The goal would be to have that person stand right next to Charlie while he continued to scarf down food treats. Next, the stimulus intensity would be raised by introducing Charlie to a more challenging individual at a distance, and so on. Then I told the McDonalds about one of my secret weapons . . . the canine halter. There was no guarantee that it would work, but it was well worth a try. The halter is usually extremely effective, particularly in retraining dogs with fearful conditions, and I had high hopes for its successful application in Charlie's case.

With a less threatening dog, I probably would have fitted the harness myself, but in Charlie's case I felt it safer all around to have the McDonalds apply the device while I directed operations from afar. I felt reasonably confident that once the halter was applied, Charlie would become much more manageable, and that I would be able to lead him. Jessie knelt down and steadied Charlie's head, and as she billed and cooed into his ear, John applied the neck strap and adjusted it to fit snugly. Then he adjusted the nose band so that Charlie could open his mouth and pant, but had it tight enough that it would not fall off the end of Charlie's snout. At this point, the loose end of the halter fell toward the ground, and I reached toward it to hand it back to John. My hand was still a foot away from Charlie's face when he whipped around with the speed of light and sank his teeth into my thumb and the back of my hand. The attack was over in a millisecond. I felt a dull, throbbing pain in my hand but made light of the incident so that Charlie didn't capitalize further on my plight and so as not to alarm the owners. Anyway, the halter was fitted, so I thought things would start to improve from there on. I wiped the blood off the back of my hand and surveyed a puncture in my thumbnail and the bluish-reddish tinge of bleeding under the nail. I knew I was going to remember Charlie for a while. I took the lead and we left through the side door, stepping onto the pavement in front of the hospital on what was a rather pleasant May afternoon. Almost as soon as we got outside, Charlie started to buck and fight the halter, scratching it with his paws, dragging his nose along the ground, and leaping from side to side like a spawning salmon.

"There's often a little struggling when you first put this device on," I assured the McDonalds. "I just have to walk him around for a while, and he should settle right into it. Come on Charlie, let's go," I said confidently, and walked briskly down the long pavement toward the parking lot, hoping that Charlie would calm down.

On the way I paused and tried to make Charlie sit by pulling up on the harness, but he simply refused. Instead he began to puff and blow, and his muscles became taut. I could see his cheeks inflating and deflating like a tree frog's throat, and then he began to salivate profusely. I persisted for a while, but Charlie only got worse.

"Why don't you have a go?" I said to John. "Perhaps I'm not the best person to be leading him along, stranger that I am."

John took his turn at leading Charlie, but nothing much changed. The dog continued to fight and struggle. Eventually we all gave up—all except Charlie! We found ourselves standing around in a circle, with Charlie in the middle of the group, discussing where to go from there. John went to hand the lead back to me, but somehow I failed to grasp the end of it and it fell on the ground. The events that followed happened unbelievably quickly, although it seemed like it was all in slow motion at the time. I realized that we couldn't leave Charlie sitting there with his lead trailing, as he was likely to take off running and busy Route 30 was only fifty yards away. Someone had to pick up the lead. It was lying nearest me. Would I be safe? I'd better try it anyway, I thought. As I bent down, reaching toward the lead, Charlie moved with the same lightning speed as before, lunging and snapping at my hand. This time he missed, but I felt the draft his jaws made across my knuckles.

"Charlie, what did you do that for?" John said as he bent down to pick up the lead himself.

He got hold of the lead for an instant, but as he went to stand up Charlie made another sudden move and bit John on the back of his hand, opening an inch-long wound. I was concerned about John, but Charlie was still loose. This time it was Jessie's turn to pick up the lead, and fortunately she managed it. I was especially grateful because by this time Charlie had my number and was walking toward me with a menacing look. Jessie was fiddling with the lead a bit and holding it rather loosely as she chattered to Charlie as though he were a naughty two-year-old who had just crayoned the wall. I stood perfectly still and instructed her to hold the lead very firmly and not to let it go. When I was certain that she had Charlie under control, I turned my attention to John and his injured hand. He needed some attention, so I took him by the arm and cautiously walked away from Jessie and Charlie, asking her to put the dog back in the car. I told her I would come back and get her later. I got John back into the consulting room, cleaned up his hand, and applied some dressings. I told him I thought he should go to the hospital and get a couple of stitches, antibiotics, and a tetanus shot, but he declined. As he sat there catching his breath we had an extracurricular conference about Charlie. Basically, John informed me that he didn't feel quite the same way about the dog as Jessie did and expressed some serious concerns about their own safety at home. The conversation was interrupted, however, as Jessie appeared at the side door. She said that she thought Charlie had been very upset by the events of the afternoon but added that he was settling down now that he was in the car.

We didn't get Charlie out of the car again; we just sat and talked for a few minutes, and Jessie reiterated her resolution to continue to work with Charlie.

"Isn't there any medication you can give him that would help him, Doctor?" Jessie asked.

"Well, there is something," I said. "We could try him on a fear-alleviating medication called propranolol that will block his fight-

or-flight response without making him drowsy. That may help him settle down a bit. I don't think it will cure Charlie, but it may reduce his aggression by as much as thirty to fifty percent, and any improvement we can make will be worthwhile."

"Can we try it?" she asked pleadingly.

"All right," I said, "but you should understand that Charlie will never be a normal dog. He will always have a problem with strangers and should be regarded as a big risk, whether he is on medication or not. The best we can hope for Charlie is that with the combination of diet, exercise, obedience training, and medication we might make him, say, fifty percent better."

"Any improvement would be welcome," she acknowledged, "and I know we have to be careful."

That's where we left it; Jessie with Charlie, her instructions, and the medication, John with a gash in his hand, and me with a throbbing thumb. I watched them drive out of the parking lot and wondered what the future held for Charlie. To my great surprise, Charlie did much better than I had predicted. After several follow-up telephone conversations with the McDonalds, we finally arrived at a point, some four months later, where Charlie was considered to be 80 percent better, and the McDonalds were absolutely thrilled. They are still in touch with me, calling up periodically to renew Charlie's prescription. The one thing it is important to know about fear conditions is that they never really go away, unless they are very mild. The best we can do is palliate the fear or desensitize the dog to some specific things, but basically the desensitization process is never over and requires constant attention. The treatment of fear by behavioral desensitization is analogous to the treatment of an allergy by a course of desensitizing injections. The allergic response to, say, bee stings can be muted by a series of desensitizing injections, but if the injections are stopped, the full-blown allergic response will once again result from a sting. It is similar with fear. Treatment is never over; it has to be an ongoing process.

If Charlie could be improved substantially by treatment, it should be possible to improve almost any fearful dog. There are many dogs I have treated for fear conditions that improve to such a great extent that the owners consider the problem "cured," reporting that their dog is "a hundred percent better" (meaning that the dog is so much better that they feel that it no longer has a problem), but on careful questioning it becomes clear that telltale signs still remain.

It is sad to see the psychological damage that can be done by mistreatment during puppyhood. The puppy's experiences, whether of abuse, neglect, or other adverse circumstances, determine the pattern of the fear that subsequently develops. The magnitude of the fear response and the form it takes depend to some extent on the dog's subsequent experiences in dealing with the fear and to some extent on the owners' reaction. Large dogs may be more intimidating and may advance more quickly through the ranks of the shy sharp biters. Owners can unwittingly escalate the fearful response by praising their dog's agitation in attempts to placate their pet. Many owners also act nervously themselves, which simply compounds the dog's fear. Owners who tense up on the lead send a message to the dog that there is trouble ahead, so that the lead becomes a kind of telegraph wire transmitting owner anxiety directly to the dog. Teaching owners to relax and provide firm direction for their dogs in the face of danger, rather than transmit their anxiety, is an important part of the prevention and treatment of fear, whether the dog is aggressive or not.

It goes without saying that the best way to deal with fear-related aggression is to prevent it from developing in the first place . . . an ounce of prevention, and all that. The training process should begin during the first week of life, before puppies have even opened their eyes. At this time, though not able to see or hear properly, puppies are still able to appreciate a human presence by touch and smell, and petting will be appreciated. Anyone who would not enjoy fostering a youngster in this way and engaging in various desensitization exercises well into the juvenile period probably should think twice about taking on a pup. Looking after pups properly is quite a commitment. The alternative is to acquire a well-balanced, already socialized dog from a shelter or pound. During such a mission it is advisable to be accompanied by someone who can knowledgeably assess canine temperament, so as to avoid acquiring a Charlie, but with this proviso, taking on a pound dog can be a rewarding experience. And, not least, you save a life.

• TREATMENT FOR •

Fear of People and Fear-Related Aggression

Dogs that are frightened of people may show avoidance behavior when young. This may subsequently develop into fear-related aggression, which is directed primarily toward strangers (especially men and children). These dogs often have a checkered history of ownership and/or socialization problems and may have had known unpleasant encounters. This type of aggression is magnified when there is no possibility of escape—for example, when the dog is on lead, chained, or in a confined space.

Treatment

1. Make sure the dog gets plenty of exercise—twenty to thirty minutes of aerobic exercise per day.
2. Feed the dog a sensible (not a performance ration) diet.
3. Start a program of regular training (with positive reinforcement only). A dog halter can be invaluable.
4. Begin desensitization and counterconditioning.
5. Avoid reinforcing the dog's fear with your own anxiety.
6. Pharmacotherapy—with drugs such as propranolol (Inderal), fluoxetine (Prozac), or buspirone (Buspar)—may be helpful.

PART III

The Obsessive/
Repetitive Dog

CHAPTER 11

Spuds & Co.

T his is the story of my involvement with the Bull Terrier
breed. Actually, it's not just a story; for me it has become a
quest, an obsession, almost a way of life.

The Bull Terrier is related to the Staffordshire (Bull) Terrier, the
American Staffordshire Terrier, and also to their infamous cousin,
the Pit Bull Terrier, but is distinguished by sometimes subtle differences in physiognomy, conformation, coloring, and stature. Bull
Terriers tend to have a markedly domed nose, small eye slits, a
barrel chest, and shortish, but not short, legs. They are usually all
white or colored (with brindle or black spotting) and weigh about
forty-five or fifty pounds when fully grown.

Despite their fighting roots, Bull Terriers are generally much
nicer than one might expect. Good ones make wonderful family
pets, as they are extremely affectionate, intelligent, and loyal, and

are such amusing characters that advocates feel that by comparison other breeds are boring. The Bull Terrier's critics, on the other hand, are quick to note that some can become extremely aggressive with minimal or no provocation, manifesting what is called rage syndrome (most of which can be accounted for by dominance), and that if they bite anyone, they tend to hang on for a while. It is said that a Bull Terrier can leap eight feet into the air, grab a tree branch with its mouth, and hang there by its teeth for twenty minutes or so, its jaws firmly locked around the branch like a vice. Detachment of the dog from its quarry can be achieved only with difficulty. (One imagines that in this situation the jaws of life, used to remove people from car wrecks, might prove to be invaluable.) Anyway, even Bull Terrier devotees agree that to be on the receiving end of an attack by one is not good fortune and is something to guard against. The hasty dispatch of dogs of this breed when they are aggressive to people—a sort of artificial selection process— probably accounts for the benign disposition of the majority of breed members. Presumably Anheuser-Busch, which inadvertently helped popularize the breed a few years ago through the Spuds MacKenzie character, learned of the breed's potential for aggression after the fact, as Spuds suddenly and mysteriously disappeared from their advertising campaign for Budweiser beer.

Bull Terriers were actually created in the early to mid-1800s by cross breeding between the English White Terrier (now extinct) and the Bulldog. Earlier versions were called the Bull *and* Terrier. Later in the nineteenth century, continued cross breeding with the English White Terrier and the Dalmation produced a strain of all-white dogs, which were called Bull Terriers. This milk-white dog became extremely fashionable in the mid- to late 1800s and acquired a sizable following. Subsequent refinements of conformation, including selection for a Roman-nosed appearance and a renewed interest in dogs with black or brindled coats ("coloreds"), brought us the Bull Terriers we know today.

My present obsession with Bull Terriers began quite unexpectedly one summer afternoon during a training class organized by a trainer who is a consultant to our behavior program, Brian Kilcommons. Various owners and assorted breeds of dog were milling around on the ball field at the veterinary school, periodically being grouped together for one or another exercise. During one of these exercises, I was paired with a Bull Terrier and its owner to instruct them on walking to heel "the Woodhouse way." Although I had always admired the unusual looks of Bull Terriers and had a healthy respect for their physical strength, I had not at that time acquired a really good feel for their personalities and did not have a good understanding of their specific behavioral traits. During a break between exercises, I chatted with the owner, David Nobriega, who, as it turns out, was a breeder. He described a problem he was experiencing with two other dogs, which he had at home, and asked me for my advice. The problem, which occurred when they were excited or stressed, involved their running in tight circles, apparently chasing their tails. I recalled a recent paper on the subject, and after the training session took David to my office, where I dug out the article and photocopied it for him. As I read the first few lines of the article to him, it struck me that the dog, which was the subject of the article, was also a young Bull Terrier, identical in almost every way to David's tail chasers. We read on together, with me imbibing every sentence of the article, which had suddenly assumed new relevance. The dog in the article responded to treatment with an endorphin-blocking drug called naloxone. This led the authors to hypothesize that Bull breeds may have an innate ability to release high levels of endorphins as part of their fighting heritage, permitting them to endure pain and somehow propagating the tail-chasing behavior—perhaps the continuous exertion of tail chasing facilitates the release of endorphins so that the behavior is intrinsically rewarding. This is not an unreasonable hypothesis, as the endorphins are part of the body's natural reward system. David and I discussed the possibility of bringing his other two dogs to the behavior clinic for examination and treatment, but this never came to pass. He left the school that day clutching his photocopy of the article and full of good intentions, but I didn't hear from the Nobriegas again for a couple of years.

The 1980s slipped away, and a new decade began. Another summer arrived. It was a hot Saturday afternoon, and I was lazing around in the front yard with the family when somewhere in the distance I thought I heard a phone ringing. As I strained my ears to locate the sound, I suddenly realized that it was my own kitchen phone, and I made a wild dash for the side door. Stumbling up the steps, I grabbed the receiver on the fifth ring.

"This is Dr. White from the Angell Memorial Animal Hospital," said a nasal voice. "Am I speaking with Dr. Dodman?"

"You are," I replied. "Do you remember me, John? We used to work together at Angell a few years back when you were doing your internship."

Dr. White, who had since become a veterinary specialist of no mean repute, acknowledged this somewhat disinterestedly, and then continued. "We have a dog here that you might be able to help us with—a young Bull Terrier that we've had in the ICU for about a week. It's been chasing its tail almost continuously, pausing briefly to eat or drink, and occasionally collapsing from exhaustion, only to resume the activity on awakening. This dog has spun so intensely that it has worn the pads off its back feet, and we have to keep them bandaged. We have run just about every test in the book and can find nothing wrong, so I've come to the conclusion that we are dealing with a behavior problem rather than a neurological disorder per se. Are you familiar with an article describing the successful treatment of a tail-chasing Bull Terrier with an endorphin-blocking drug?"

"I am," I replied.

"Well, I've costed out that treatment from our pharmacy, and it will set the owners back about three hundred and fifty dollars for a test injection, which will only last about twenty minutes. Do you have any research supplies of that drug that we can try on this dog? If so, how can we get hold of them?"

I realized that it was my facilities rather than my faculties that were in demand, but in light of my interest in the condition, I was happy to oblige.

"Why don't you send the dog out here, John?" I suggested. "I'd like to monitor the response myself."

He agreed, and the owners, Rob and Brenda Murdoch, were soon on their way from Boston with their five-month-old male Bull Terrier, Teddy. While they were in transit, I called the pharmacy at the veterinary school and asked the pharmacist to make up an injection of naltrexone, a more potent and longer-lasting endorphin-blocking drug than the one that had been employed in the case report. Putting family life on hold for a short while, I ran down and picked up the injection, arriving back at the house shortly before the Murdochs. They were a young childless couple, and Teddy was their pride and joy. They hadn't just acquired him on a whim; they had spent months researching the type of dog they would like before selecting Teddy some two months earlier. He had been a perfect family member for the first month, everything they had wished for and dreamed of, but in the second month some mild, desultory spinning had been noticed. This had suddenly worsened a week earlier for no apparent reason. The local veterinarian had referred them to Angell Memorial Animal Hospital, and that's where Dr. White had taken over.

The couple stood in front of me, emotionally drained and obviously distraught. Rob clutched the struggling Teddy tightly to his chest. After a brief introduction, I invited Rob to put Teddy down on the kitchen floor so that I could observe the behavior. Teddy ran around and around in tight circles, chasing but never catching his tail. He appeared to be in an extremely excited state and was howling and barking hysterically as he bounced off walls, chairs, and the legs of the kitchen table. It was a pathetic sight, and I prayed that the injection would work, providing the poor creature with some relief from his affliction. There was no time to explain fully the rationale underlying the proposed treatment, but elevating my voice over the ruckus, I attempted an abbreviated explanation of what was to be done. First, my wife, also a veterinarian, assisted me in placing an intravenous catheter into a vein in the dog's front leg. Then I slowly injected the colorless solution into a port in the catheter, explaining to the Murdochs that it might be a few minutes before we saw an effect. Teddy was confined in a recess off the kitchen by means of a kiddy gate while I grabbed a camcorder to film the ensuing events. The camera rolled, but Teddy continued to spin and bark. The Murdochs stood expressionless as we waited for the miracle cure. The final result: not even the slightest change in the dog's behavior. Ten minutes after the injection, I had to acknowledge that the treatment had been unsuccessful. Tears rolled down Brenda's face as the couple contemplated their options. My wife and I pondered the failure of the treatment. We gazed at Teddy spinning as we did so, racking our brains for a solution. After a short while, my wife said, "You know, it looks an awful lot as if he's having some kind of seizure." I had to agree. The howling, the running, the detachment, and the dissociation did give the impression that Teddy was something less than fully conscious. He certainly appeared to be undergoing some sort of electrical brainstorm.

"Maybe he would respond to an intravenous injection of Valium, like a dog having a full-blown epileptic seizure," I ventured.

Would the Murdochs go for it? They had already been through so much. I tried to explain that the information gained from Teddy's response to Valium would help not only Teddy but also the breed in general by adding to our understanding of the condition. The Murdochs agreed to the injection as a last-ditch measure. Rob held Teddy as I trickled the viscous, straw-colored Valium solution into Teddy's vein. The countdown began. As if by magic, Teddy began to relax within two minutes of the injection. The barking stopped, the involuntary movements stopped, and you could almost see the relief spread across his face. He began to wag his tail, then turned toward his master and began licking his face affectionately. Our jaws dropped as we observed this minor miracle. Rob cautiously lowered Teddy to the ground, and Teddy proceeded to walk in straight lines, although a little drunkenly, and finally sat down, head cocked to one side, panting slightly, apparently wondering what came next. As we savored the fruits of victory, Teddy began to glance anxiously over his left shoulder and to display an unhealthy interest in his tail and nether regions. The situation deteriorated as he made floundering attempts to grasp his tail, and the behavior slowly returned. Subsequent shots of Valium had a similar effect to the first, but, as before, the quenching effect was only transient. I suggested to the Murdochs that they might like to book Teddy into our ICU for a few days for stabilization on longer-lasting anticonvulsants, but they were emotionally (and financially) drained, and decided at this point to throw in the towel. They both cried as Teddy received an injection of euthanasia solution and sank peacefully to sleep in their arms. It was a very bad time to ask them whether we could perform a postmortem, but I did anyway. They declined, preferring to take Teddy home to be buried in their backyard. They thanked me for my trouble, and I helped them load Teddy into the trunk of the car. The sad couple drove off down the road, and as I watched them disappear I found myself wishing for the opportunity to come face to face with another case of this abominable condition so that I could test what I thought might be a successful treatment.

Months passed and the winter came. It was around nine o'clock one weeknight when I received yet another call from a distraught Bull Terrier owner, Richard Johnson from Rhode Island. His dog, Brandy, had a history almost identical to Teddy's. The dog was a young male of about six months of age and had started spinning only a few days before. Richard had found out about me from the Nobriegas, and I spoke with them and with Brandy's breeder, Dawn Mednick, before the night was out. We all were extremely interested in finding out more about Brandy's condition and how to treat it, and Richard agreed to deliver Brandy to the veterinary school the following day for evaluation. The Johnsons arrived at the hospital early the next morning. I started the consultation with Brandy present, but because of his constant hysterical howling and circling, I had to have him removed immediately to the ICU, where he was treated with serial injections of Valium. The Valium had the desired effect, and by the time the Johnsons left an hour later,

Brandy was quite calm, although a little drunk. I took a detailed behavioral history from the Johnsons and obtained their signed consent to keep Brandy in the ICU for a few days under close observation. They also authorized me to perform a full neurological examination, including an electroencephalogram and a CT scan. The expense involved in this was considerable, but the Johnsons resolved to stay the course to help poor Brandy and find out what was wrong.

The following day, Brandy was anesthetized and taken to the electrophysiology room for an electroencephalogram. We used a full set of electrodes in order to better localize the problem and applied visual, auditory, and mechanical challenges in order to reveal any subtle abnormal electrical activity in the dog's brain. The whole spectacle looked like a scene from *Young Frankenstein,* with the strobe light flickering in a room full of electrical equipment and with the dog, decked in a Medusa's head of wires, the focus of our attention. I don't know whether I expected to get positive findings or not, since you don't always find something when you run an EEG, even in cases of grand mal seizures, but I do remember the excitement of discovery when the recording pens produced a series of spikes characteristic of epilepsy. Eureka! We were thrilled by the finding. We now had a much firmer diagnosis and some hope that we could perhaps engineer a successful treatment. Brandy, still under anesthesia, was trundled through to the CT scan on a gurney, and the hourlong radiographic brain imaging began. We were all still too excited about the EEG to be paying much attention to the CT scan, but it wasn't long before I was summoned to the CT scan control room, where the radiologist calmly pointed out that Brandy also had hydrocephalus, an excess accumulation of fluid within the brain. This revelation caused yet more excitement, more feverish conversations, more theories and speculation. But what did it all mean? How did it all fit together? We knew we had discovered something, but we weren't sure what.

The day after the EEG and CT scan, Brandy was treated first with an endorphin-blocking drug and later with a long acting anticonvulsant. As before, the endorphin-blocking drug had no obvious effect, while the anticonvulsant, given intravenously, stopped Brandy from spinning and made him much calmer. He was kept in the hospital for a few more days, and his condition stabilized on an oral form of the anticonvulsant. On the last day of this five-day stay, he hardly circled at all, and we felt that his future looked quite rosy. The Johnsons arrived late in the afternoon to pick him up, and although we had hoped that he would impress them with his composure, the excitement of seeing them was too much, and he started spinning wildly. Back to the ICU we went, where more Valium was given intravenously and intramuscularly to get him under control for the journey home. The Johnsons were also given a few hundred Valium pills to be given to Brandy as needed to control any future breakthroughs of the spinning behavior.

I had several conversations with the Johnsons over the following two weeks, and although there were a few relapses, it appeared that Brandy's condition was finally coming under control. It was then that the aggression started. During his now less-frequent spinning bouts, which were precipitated by the arrival of guests, he would become indiscriminately aggressive, biting at people near him or even inanimate objects such as doors or chairs. The Johnsons became unnerved—and rightfully so, bearing in mind the damage that "Bullies" can inflict. Primarily for safety reasons, they returned Brandy to his breeder, Dawn Mednick, who graciously refunded their money and agreed to work with Brandy herself. By this time, we were treating Brandy with three different anticonvulsants; as the weeks passed, there didn't seem to be any further improvement in his condition. Dawn sought a second opinion about Brandy from a board-certified neurologist in New Hampshire, and while he agreed with the diagnosis, he felt that the prognosis was poor. It turns out that this was an accurate prediction, because Brandy bit Dawn in the hand as she attempted to get him back into her car, and on her return she elected to have him euthanized. Dawn was an official of the Genetic Defects Committee of the Bull Terrier Club of America and had more than a passing interest in this condition. She knew that we would have to have a postmortem examination performed if we were to learn more about this enigmatic condition. As difficult as it was for her, she bravely brought poor Brandy to the veterinary school, where he was humanely euthanized and subsequently autopsied.

All this time, I was avidly reading everything I could about Bull Terriers, genetic disease, hydrocephalus, and whatever else seemed relevant to the case. I located one extremely interesting article describing an inherited condition of Bull Terriers that manifests itself at a young age as severe dermatitis, failure to thrive, an increased susceptibility to infections, and eventually to death. The condition, called lethal acrodermatitis, was thought to be due to an inherited problem with zinc metabolism, and affected pups showed seizure-like activity, increased aggressiveness, and hydrocephalus. Could we be dealing with a different manifestation of the same problem? If so, how would we prove it? The postmortem examination on Brandy indicated skin disease, hydrocephalus, and kidney disease. The skin disease certainly fit with the zinc-deficiency-syndrome theory, being of the same type as that described in the zinc-deficient pups. I elected to have an expert neuropathologist, Dr.

Rod Bronson, look at specific brain areas for changes characteristic of zinc-deficiency seizures, and I explained the whole story to him. In the course of the discussion, Dr. Bronson remarked that the previous director of his laboratory had been a zinc specialist who had left him numerous publications on the subject. He also recalled a publication regarding a particular strain of zinc-deficient mice, which would spin in circles on account of zinc-induced changes in the balance organs of the inner ear. Needless to say, zinc-deficiency syndromes, including those affecting zinc-deficient mice, became our next focus of interest. A review of the literature on the subject indicated that zinc deficiency can cause hydrocephalus, seizures, and inner-ear problems, as well as skin problems and problems with the immune system, increasing susceptibility to infection. The zinc deficiency hypothesis became more compelling with each new turn.

Although detailed brain pathology was inconclusive in Brandy's case, our deliberations led us to believe that the whole complex of behavioral and organic changes could be related to zinc deficiency. Another expert was contacted because of his interest in and understanding of zinc deficiency and its manifestations. This individual, Dr. Lawrence Erway, from the University of Cincinnati and the Bar Harbor Laboratory in Maine, concurred with our developing theories about a genetic link and remarked that he was surprised that the Bull Terrier breed, unlike white cats and Dalmatian dogs, did not suffer from a deafness problem as well. And as a matter of fact they do. I began to wonder how many of the breed's common problems, ranging from cleft palate to umbilical hernia, heart disease, kidney disease, and slipping knee caps, could be explained by a single genetic defect in zinc metabolism. The answer was that they all could, but who would believe it and where should we go from here?

The next piece of the puzzle was supplied by our dermatologist at the veterinary school, who recalled a collaborative study between a veterinarian and a human-nutrition researcher at the University of California at Davis. These scientists had measured zinc and copper in blood samples from Bull Terriers with lethal acrodermatitis. The veterinarian involved in the study had subsequently departed academia for a life in private practice, but I was able to reach him and, through him, finally managed to track down the nutritionist, Dr. Keene. Dr. Keene was extremely interested and helpful and agreed to share his results on lethal acrodermatitis and to work with us to investigate the new theory. He volunteered the services of his laboratory for analysis of tissue levels of various metals, including zinc and copper, and brainstormed with me about the underlying genetic disturbance and the possible role of a zinc transporter protein called metallothionine. My colleague at the medical school in Boston, Dr. Louis Shuster, was also becoming more involved in the project as time went by, and he agreed to assay the blood and tissues of affected dogs for metallothionine.

Thanks to the assistance of a few dedicated local breeders, the next several months saw the gradual acquisition of data from both normal Bull Terriers and dogs affected with either lethal acrodermatitis or the spinning problem. We are still chewing over these results which will get published one day as soon as we have cleaned up the definitions of the behaviors themselves. One of the spinning dogs, Posie, was another of Dawn's stock, which she had sold to a family on Long Island, New York. Within days of arriving in her new home, Posie began to spin and had to be returned to Massachusetts. Dawn brought her to our hospital for the full neurological workup, and, as with all the other spinners, the EEG revealed brain activity characteristic of epilepsy and a CT scan showed a fairly severe degree of hydrocephalus. Posie was successfully treated with the anticonvulsant phenobarbital and was eventually returned to her new owners in Long Island. Unfortunately, the stress of the move caused her to start spinning right away, so she was brought back to her New England home and is presently maintaining a spin-free life on a low dose of an anticonvulsant.

At about this time, the Welfare Foundation of the Bull Terrier Club of America had been informed of our ongoing research and they made some funds available to me so that owners could have their dogs fully evaluated without breaking the bank. I felt very comfortable dealing with the secretary of the foundation, as he and I had been at Glasgow University together in the late 1960s, and no doubt had frequented the same haunts in our undergraduate years. Through conversations with the secretary and Dawn Mednick, I became more aware of the inner workings of the Bull Terrier Club of America, and the format of its annual meeting, called Silverwood. I became aware that not all the members of the club were equally enthused about the prospect of pushing forward with research into the problems of the breed. There were those who adopted the philosophy that all breeds have problems and probably always will, so why do anything? There were others who took the opposite view, that it was reprehensible to breed from genetically defective stock. Luckily for me, the latter proponents were extremely vocal, probably because of direct experience with problem dogs. Eventually I made the acquaintance of the vice president of the breed club, who invited me to speak at the annual Silverwood meeting in 1993, and I accepted, even though the findings were quite preliminary at the time.

As the meeting drew closer, I continued my research into pedigrees, but ran into some difficulties as breed politics became more of a factor. I was advised by a colleague that the actual names of the affected dogs should remain secret if I wanted to garner support. It was a little unnerving to come face to face with the politics of the situation and at the same time to have the hypothesis veering slightly as the meeting loomed. I felt like a sacrificial lamb on the road to slaughter. I had noted that some of the dogs discussed in the published lethal acrodermatitis paper had experienced a coat color change from black to bronze. The only explanation for this was a simultaneous deficiency in copper. This could fit in with the zinc-deficiency hypothesis as a secondary phenomenon, but it could also be that copper deficiency was the primary deficiency with zinc secondarily involved. Our laboratory results were pointing more in the latter direction. All I could do was be honest and pray for an understanding audience.

The big day finally came. I flew to Chicago's O'Hare Airport and caught a limo to the hotel that was the venue for the Bull Terrier Club's annual meeting. As I reached the hotel gate I was astounded to see scores of Bull Terriers milling around in the parking lot. My presentation was at one o'clock, so I found a quiet corner of the hotel and glanced through my slides. When the time came to speak, I began my talk with Brandy's story and then branched out into my theories regarding the causes of his condition. I felt that the bulk of the audience was with me, despite the complexity of the subject matter, but I was acutely aware of a couple of ardent dissenters. At the end of the presentation I received a warm round of applause, and after answering a slew of questions from the floor, I made a hasty exit, wanting to get back to Boston in time to get a decent night's sleep. A small group met me at the door and fired a final series of questions at me as I left the meeting. I knew that I had raised more issues than I had resolved, but at least I had made an impression. The "Spuds Project" was up and running.

Since the meeting, many Bull Terriers have been referred to me from all over the country. Some of them were tail chasers and some suffered from rage syndrome, but others had a different problem—compulsive ball playing or log carrying—which has put a new complexion on the subject. Although at first glance these latter behaviors don't seem to be related to tail chasing but, on reflection, a compulsion to chase and grasp a tail is not a far cry from a compulsion directed toward a tennis ball or a log. Accordingly, I have begun to view many of these behaviors as possibly being *seizure-induced compulsive behaviors*. This new classification permits a more meaningful look at the inheritance of the condition, which is one of the directions that I am hotly pursuing with the help of a new addition to the staff of the behavior section, behavioral geneticist Dr. Alice Moon. Alice drew my attention to the fact that the compulsive behaviors of Bull Terriers bore many resemblances to innate predatory behavior. This made a lot of sense, as in the early days of the breed Bull Terriers were selectively inbred to enhance their predatory tendencies. More specifically, pit-fighting and rat-killing abilities were highly valued, so that dogs that excelled in either of these behaviors were championed and bred. According to the earliest book published on Bull Terriers, one particularly successful rat-killer killed several hundred rats in an hour. Now that's what I call serious predation.

The way our theory has evolved now is that we believe we may be dealing with an inherited disorder of metallic ion metabolism, which causes partial (behavioral) seizures with an epicenter somewhere in the limbic region of the brain (the center that controls emotions). Seizures or seizure-like activity in this region cause extreme fluctuations of mood, ranging from rage to extreme fear—both of which I have seen—and may also trigger one or more innate, hard-wired behaviors encoded in the nearby basal ganglia. The result of this is the compulsion to perform certain behaviors repetitively and out of context. Interestingly, humans with obsessive-compulsive disorder also have abnormal brain geometry, and some have a concomitant seizure disorder. The newly expanded theory is not simply food for academic thought; it has lead to new treatment strategies. Recently, Alice and I have been using the human antiobsessional drug Prozac (and its look-alikes) to complement treatment with anticonvulsants in affected dogs. This has led to a tremendous increase in our treatment success rate, and dogs like Brandy now stand a better chance of a cure than ever before. We continue to build on our theory with a view to refining diagnosis and treatment even further. One of our most important goals is to enable breeders to identify susceptible dogs so that, in time, it may be possible to eliminate the problem by selective breeding. Along these lines, so called linkage studies are planned for the near future in the hopes of identifying a genetic marker. If we are successful in our quest it may soon be possible to identify subclinically affected and carrier dogs by looking at cells collected from within the dog's cheek by means of a cutip that would really lift the fog enveloping ethical breeding strategies and pave the way forward. If we were really lucky this work could lead to the discovery of the gene (or genes) responsible for the condition. And that would be that. Case closed. Ain't science wonderful?

• TREATMENT FOR •

Compulsive Behavior of Bull Terriers

Various compulsive behaviors are shown by this breed, including tail chasing and obsessive behavior toward toys, logs, tennis balls, and so on. The behavior may well be a canine form of obsessive-compulsive disorder and appears to be associated with partial seizure activity in the brain.

Diagnosis and Diagnostic Criteria

1. Observation and quantitation of the behavior. Does it occupy more than 1 hour per day? Does it interfere with normal activities? Does the dog become anxious when restrained from performing the behavior?
2. EEG—fast activity, epileptiform spiking
3. CT—hydrocephalus (not invariably present)
4. Response to anticonvulsant or antiobsessional drug—compulsive behavior lessens or ceases

Treatment

1. Try to provide the dog with as diverse and interesting an environment as possible. Minimize the use of a crate and other forms of confinement, and minimize the time the dog spends alone.
2. Provide as much exercise as possible and change to an appropriate diet.
3. Train the dog to perform behaviors that are incompatible with the unwanted behavior (counterconditioning).
4. Medicate the dog with anticonvulsants such as phenobarbital or antiobsessional drugs such as Prozac (fluoxetine) under the direction of a veterinarian.

CHAPTER 12

Shadow of a Doubt

I n the early days of the behavior program at the Tufts veterinary school, I used to field all of the telephone inquiries about behavior problems myself because no one else was available. To put it into pack perspective, I was both the alpha and omega. Arriving at work to find fifteen or twenty telephone messages from desperate owners was daunting at times, but I rolled up my sleeves and got on with it. One of the challenges I constantly faced was trying to decipher what the problem was from the owner's description of the behavior. Sometimes it was possible to make a fairly accurate diagnosis over the phone, but other times it was not so easy. One of the not-so-easy variety involved an Old English Sheepdog that was supposed to be hallucinating about rabbits. The call came from Angie Warren of the Old English Sheepdog Club Rescue Service. Angie was trying to place Brendan, the dog in question, in a new home but was finding the task difficult because of some very odd behavior he exhibited. Angie could only describe the behavior as "chasing imaginary rabbits around her house until they eventually disappeared down imaginary rabbit holes."

"Rabbits . . . ," I mused, wondering which one of the three of us was hallucinating.

Actually, although Angie was dead serious in her description of the behavior, she knew a lot more than she was letting on at first and was simply having a little fun at my expense. Brendan's problem was the first of many cases of shadow chasing that I would encounter over the next few years. Angie agreed to bring Brendan to the hospital for an examination, and meanwhile sent me reams of information about him. He had been picked up by the New England Old English Sheepdog Club Rescue Service from a Rhode Island pound earlier in the year. His previous owners were in the process of a divorce and had left him at a boarding kennel in Rhode Island, where he had lived for a while alongside a greyhound. He was turned over to the pound when the owners refused to pick him up or pay their bill. Angie had called the delinquent owners, who filled her in on Brendan's earlier history but didn't want him back. The essential facts were that Brendan was a three-and-a-half-year-old, eighty-pound Old English Sheepdog and was as deaf as a post. He was one of eleven pups and apparently had been quite ill when he was six weeks old, requiring intensive care for a gastrointestinal problem. He recovered from this bout and turned into a very sweet though difficult pup. Early on in his life his owners started playing with him by shining a flashlight on the floor. Brendan loved this game and chased the flashlight beam frantically. Soon, however, it became more than a game for Brendan, turning into an obsession that totally consumed him. He began chasing sunbeams, shadows, and even things that (to us) weren't there.

Brendan's deafness was first noticed by a trainer sometime during the first year of his life and confirmed by specialists at Angell Memorial Animal Hospital. Even at this time, Brendan had to be given Valium to calm him down during moments of stress, so he was far from well, temperamentally speaking. He had been taken to another behaviorist, a colleague of mine, who taught him hand signals. She also discussed the use of a Tabasco-and-water spray directed into his mouth as aversive therapy for the shadow chasing. The owners could not comply with this latter advice because they thought it was mean, so they used lemon juice instead, but it didn't work. The behaviorist then suggested a greyhound companion for Brendan, to remind him of earlier happy times, but this strategy met with no success, as Brendan and the greyhound fought over food. A short course of some medication was also tried, but to no avail. Now it was my turn to get involved with this case and see what I could do.

Angie brought Brendan to the veterinary school one September day in 1989, and we all got to know each other. Angie is one of those high-energy, intelligent people who don't miss a trick. Her bright eyes darted back and forth between Brendan and me as we went over some of the details of his behavior. Brendan seemed quite calm as he peered at me from beneath his long bangs. I noticed that one of his eyes was pale blue and was a so-called wall eye—which was not that exceptional in a dog with gray and white harlequin coloring. Both the wall eye and the coat color are a result of uneven pigment distribution, and in all likelihood, so was his deafness problem. The pigment, melanin, is needed for the normal neural development of the inner ear. Apparently pigment cells migrate to the ear during development, paving the way for nerve cells that follow in their wake. If unpigmented areas coincide with areas in which auditory development is taking place, faulty nerve development and thus deafness can be the result. The same thing happens in human beings with Wardenburg syndrome. Affected individuals, who have a shock of white hair, often have deafness problems too.

As I reflected on these issues, wondering about the significance of the deafness, Angie continued to bombard me with facts about Brendan. She informed me that she had previously placed him with a young couple who were prepared to accept his shadow chasing, but they had returned him when he bit one of them as they tried to load him into a crate. I figured that this was probably because of dominance-related aggression, which is not uncommon in Old English Sheepdogs. The couple returned Brendan after four days, and after a brief stay in a foster home, he ended up back with Angie. When he first arrived back in Angie's home, he was well behaved and calm and seemed quite content in a smallish indoor pen. He was peaceful like this for about three or four days but then began to revert to his old shadow-chasing self.

Initially Brendan had spells when he would become overly active and dart around his pen, pausing occasionally to stare at shadows he cast on the wall behind him. Soon the behavior became so intense that it was Brendan's only activity, barring eating and sleeping. He never sat or lay still and was, basically, in perpetual motion. Angie had tried putting a blanket in front of his pen to block the shadows, and this helped quite a bit. With the blanket up to prevent shadows, Brendan calmed down considerably and spent at least some of the time chewing on a nylon bone or peeking around the blanket at Angie. He continued, however, to stare out of the pen at where the shadows used to be, and though this occupied quite a lot of his time, it was a welcome relief from the shadow chasing. Sometimes Brendan would scratch at the floor, as if digging for something, when there was nothing there, but he seemed to be having fun. His excuse-for-a-tail would wag while he was digging, and the whole thing appeared to be a bit of a game. After about a week, Angie removed the blanket to see what would happen, and Brendan immediately returned to shadow chasing. It became apparent that people approaching the pen were a trigger for his shadow chasing, apparently because they cast shadows. Eventually, Brendan could be approached only from one side of his cage, where, because of the lighting, there were no shadows cast.

Following the blanket experiment, Angie tried treating Brendan with extra-large doses of tender loving care, petting him for long periods of time to stop him from chasing shadows. This sometimes had the desired effect, but in general he didn't seem to like the petting as much as the chance to get that shadow. He got so used to having her attention, though, that at times he even came up to her and rubbed against her like a cat, asking for his back rub. During the day he spent a lot of time staring at Angie, watching her in her daily activities and watching other dogs come and go. He was very friendly with the other dogs and was submissive in play, never trying to dominate the others. Sometimes he would stop in the middle of a submissive roll on the floor with another dog to chase something that he thought (or hoped) was a shadow. His mind seemed never to be completely free of thoughts of shadows.

Another behavioral treatment Angie had tried was to catch Brendan's eye periodically during the day and wave at him, then approach him to give him a hug and a pat. It was just another way of trying to strengthen the bond between person and dog when sounds cannot be included in the communication repertoire. Other people visiting the home were also told of this signal, and Brendan responded reasonably well to this new interaction, pausing more frequently to catch people's eyes and receive his reward. Brendan became quite good at interpreting various hand signals and understood signs for "Sit," "Down," "Stay," "No," "Quiet," and "Good boy." He seemed really happy when he had done something right, and was so excited by the sign for "Good boy" that he acted as though he were going to explode.

Angie told me that Brendan loved to ride in the car. He never searched for shadows or chased them while inside a car, and could stay there all day long and be perfectly happy. Some sheep-herding dogs are not so calm in this situation; they appear to view other vehicles as rapidly moving sheep. This causes great consternation (particularly at five-way intersections!) and can be hazardous for the driver. Brendan was just the opposite, and sometimes when he was excited, putting him in the car would have an effect like a tranquilizer, causing him to fall asleep within five minutes. I wondered what this meant and whether it could be used to advantage during the treatment program.

One other factor that was becoming progressively more apparent with Brendan was that he was constantly testing the person in charge of him. Firm control was always necessary, and if Brendan didn't have a strong leader, he would assume control himself. Angie even reported that Brendan had challenged her on a couple of occasions, once when she was trying to keep control of him with a leash and once when she went to put him in his crate. His modus operandi was that he would growl and bare his teeth or turn around and try to grab an arm. On one occasion he even charged Angie. These incidents, which occurred whenever Brendan was prevented from doing what he wanted to do, suggested a dominance-related problem. Although this behavior was of concern, and potentially serious, it wasn't the immediate problem at hand, so I didn't get into it as much as I could have.

After our interview, I asked Angie to bring Brendan to an observation room, where I attempted to elicit and film the shadow chasing. Angie was quite confident that Brendan would perform if left alone, but just in case he was distracted by the new environment, she brought a flashlight, which she felt certain would get him going. At first Brendan just nosed around the periphery of the room, paying little attention to us as he explored his new environment. After five minutes or so we were both a little tired of waiting, so we decided to expedite things by using the flashlight. That did it! Instantly Brendan leaped toward the illuminated area, then fell into a play bow and stared at the illuminated spot. Angie quickly zipped the beam across the room away from the dog. He followed it so quickly and closely, it was almost as if he were attached to the beam by a string. Wherever the beam ended up, he was sure to arrive two nanoseconds later. It was tiring just watching Brendan charging about, so once I had enough of the behavior on tape I asked Angie to turn off the flashlight. She gave me an elfish look as she did it because she knew what was going to happen next. Brendan continued as if nothing had changed. He was charging around the room from one side to the other, essentially chasing nothing, occasionally stopping and staring at a particular point in the floor (the rabbit hole!). Eventually we had to physically restrain him by putting on his lead and taking him out of the room.

"Pretty weird, isn't it?" said Angie. I had to agree.

We put Brendan back in the car, where we knew he would be peaceful, and started to discuss what was going on and what the treatment options were. Angie told me that she had come across three other Old English Sheepdogs with this condition before, so I asked her to rack her brain to see if there were any things they had in common, aside from breed. She remembered that two of the other dogs had also been deaf, although she wasn't sure about the third. I got to thinking that deafness might be a factor and wondered whether all shadow chasers were deaf. It seemed to make sense that visual experiences would be more exhilarating for a dog that could not hear, so this was a reasonable premise. I still think deafness may be a factor in some dogs, although I have subsequently come across other shadow chasers that can hear perfectly well.

Other factors I carefully considered were Brendan's hyperactivity and perseverance. He was certainly a bundle of energy, and seemed incapable of disengaging from the behavior once it had been initiated. I began to think that behavioral and medical treatments designed to reduce anxiety and instill calmness might be beneficial. Then again, his inability to disengage from the behavior brought to mind the possibility of a seizure-based phenomenon. The initial treatment plan included adequate exercise, a balanced, low-protein diet, and behavior-modification therapy in which his shadow chasing was ignored while any quiet periods were rewarded with attention and treats. Angie was also asked to continue to ensure good communication through obedience training with hand signals. In addition, Brendan was medicated with an anxiety-reducing drug, Tranxene, which is similar to Valium. Tranxene also has anticonvulsant properties, so I hoped the problem could be controlled one way or the other.

But it wasn't to be. The medication sedated him to the point of making him uncoordinated and shaky, while at the same time it made him ravenously hungry. He became so hungry that he began eating the cat's litter, paper, and almost anything else he could find. His shadow-chasing behavior remained virtually unchanged, however. I switched to an anticonvulsant, phenobarbital, in the hope that this medication might produce results, but once again nothing happened. I ceased all medication after that and concentrated on a few of the techniques that Angie had found successful in the past. With these strategies—the blanket, the hand signals, the petting, and the positive reinforcement of good behavior—we were beginning to make some headway. But progress was slow.

As I continued to scratch my head about Brendan, I got a disturbing phone call from Angie. She told me that she had to have Brendan put to sleep because he had bitten her. Angie had reached down to Brendan's collar to bring him into the house, and without warning he turned and bit her badly, leaving a deep puncture wound. Brendan had shown no remorse and even began to stalk her. Angie had to grab a shovel to defend herself. At that point she knew there was no way that the two of them could continue together, and she had made the only decision she could. I was disappointed for Angie because I knew she had tried so hard; I was disappointed for Brendan; and I felt a little guilty myself about having concentrated so hard on the shadow-chasing aspects of his behavior, paying insufficient attention to the dominance issue that ultimately brought about his untimely demise.

While I was brooding about Brendan's fate, I was contacted by the owner of yet another shadow chasing dog. The back-to-back appearance of these two cases provided a great opportunity for comparison. The next case, Cullie, was a one-year-old spayed female Rottweiler-Labrador cross; she looked like a pure Rottweiler except for her small stature. Cullie had been taken from her mother at the age of four weeks. When she was nine months old, her owner, Josie Kenney, noticed that she jumped at and chased a few shadows. At the time, she thought it was "cute puppy play" and actually encouraged the behavior during regular play periods. About ten days after the behavior first emerged, the cuteness disappeared, and Josie knew she had a real problem on her hands. Cullie became obsessed with shadows cast by any moving object. The obsession became so severe that for three days she had to be hand fed what little she ate, and the weight just dropped off her before her anxious owner's eyes. Constant movement was the rule, at least until everyone was in bed at night and the lights were out. Josie had already taken Cullie to her local veterinarian, who hadn't been able to help her although he had run just about every test in the book. No physical or functional abnormality was found. As an interim measure, the veterinarian had treated Cullie with phenobarbital, which seemed to calm her somewhat. Josie reported that without it, Cullie was a basket case. Even with the drug, however, she was still far from a normal dog.

Cullie was different from Brendan—she was a different breed and sex, and she had good hearing. The only similarities were that she had been separated from her mother rather early and rather abruptly when she was a pup, and she had been encouraged to perform the behavior in early life, when it seemed like fun. I was intrigued by the fact that low-dose phenobarbital had appeared to have some beneficial effects in Cullie, but thought that I would try a purely behavioral strategy to start. I had the owners focus more intently on attention withdrawal during the dog's shadow-chasing bouts, working on the theory that the behavior might be exacerbated by the owners' attention, good or bad. I recommended that Cullie should be actively avoided at times when she was engaging in the behavior. I also advised Josie to use what is termed a *bridging stimulus*. A bridging stimulus is a neutral stimulus designed to interrupt and focus a dog's attention prior to initiating some response. In Cullie's case, I advised the use of a duck call as the bridging stimulus, although any low-pitched note, such as that made by a tuning fork or striking a key on a piano, would have done just as well. Josie was to make the low sound whenever she saw Cullie chasing shadows, then turn around immediately and walk away. The theory was that Cullie's attention would be focused by the sound and that the next event she noticed would be Josie leaving. If successful, this would be an example of negative reinforcement at work. Simply put, Cullie would stop shadow chasing to avoid an unpleasant (negative) event: Josie's leaving.

Several weeks later, I heard back from Josie. The results had been spectacular. Although Cullie wasn't cured, her behavior was very much improved. Josie felt that there had been an 80 percent decrease in Cullie's shadow-chasing behavior. I stayed in touch with Josie for some time, and each time we spoke, Cullie's behavior was further improved. Eventually she no longer chased shadows— indoors at least. Josie reported that when Cullie was outside, particularly as the sun set and cast long shadows on the lawn, she would occasionally run around and indulge in her old fetish, but she hastened to add that she had never trained Cullie outside. Both Josie and I were very pleased at the results of the behavior modification, and as far as Josie was concerned, the problem was solved.

I continued to wonder what was driving the mysterious condition of shadow chasing. I now knew that it could be reinforced by the owners' attention, but what caused it in the first place? Was it simply learned by chance? Was there some kind of innate tendency for the behavior? Or was there some obscure environmental influence? I still don't have all the answers, but I have one or two thoughts on the matter that may prove illuminating. The first occurred when I was consulted by the owner of a Bull Terrier. This owner reported that at the age of six months, her dog had started to chase shadows along a wall, at first in a desultory way and then continuously and to the exclusion of everything else. These shadows became a complete obsession to the point where, at the local vet's suggestion, the dog was euthanized. What I knew about Bull Terriers and their inherited tendency toward partial (behavioral) seizures made me more suspicious that seizures were somehow involved in the behavior. Alternatively, obsessive-compulsive behaviors that may be associated with such seizures in Bull Terriers might also be responsible. After all, some human obsessive-compulsive sufferers have an underlying seizure problem. In Bull Terriers, the usual compulsions (tail chasing, ball fetishes, and so on) seem to be related to predatory behavior, and it seems pretty clear that shadow chasing is also a form of predatory behavior. Only additional cases and studies of their response to specific treatments will clarify this matter.

The second experience that caused me to think about seizures as a cause was an encounter with a fly-catching pup. This young dog snapped at imaginary flies, and once this curious behavior began, the animal would continue to the point of exhaustion. The similarities between this condition and shadow chasing were remarkable. The behavior was initially encouraged by the owners' snapping their fingers over the dog's head—this has been the case with all the fly-catching dogs that I have seen. This dog (and the other fly-catching dogs) also seemed to have had a fairly dull existence, suffering from what I call sensory deprivation syndrome. For this dog

I attempted the same bridging stimulus–attention withdrawal treatment that I had tried with Cullie and had the same success, confirming an attention-getting component in the behavior. Interestingly, fly catching is also thought to be associated with behavioral seizures, and appears for all the world to be another example of predatory behavior gone awry.

Shadow chasing, fly catching, and many other apparently hallucinatory behaviors thus seem to have many features in common. They start when the dog is young; they are encouraged by the owners; the dogs often have no useful function to perform and spend a good deal of their time confined. The breeds affected (from Miniature Schnauzers to Bull Terriers) are no strangers to the seizure scene, although the seizures that may be involved are not of the grand mal type. Obsessive-compulsive behavior, which also seems an adequate explanation for these behaviors, is sometimes associated with partial seizures as well, making a curious mix. As might be expected, the breeds that show this behavior also tend to have strong predatory instincts: my last two cases were a Wire-Haired Fox Terrier and a field-strain Labrador. Maybe shadow chasing and fly catching are just novel ways (albeit based in the predatory instinct) in which dogs manifest obsessive-compulsive disorder. I am now trying antiobsessional drugs to complement behavioral therapy for shadow-chasing dogs, and they seem to be at least partially effective. The Wire-Haired Fox Terrier is 50 percent better after four weeks of Prozac and counting. This little fellow and the Labrador would chase shadows even when there was no one around, so wanting attention wasn't the only reason for their behavior.

Whatever the full explanation may turn out to be, I have come a long way toward understanding more about this behavior compared to when I was first told about the imaginary rabbits and rabbit holes. I know better where I need to look and what treatments might be effective, and I'm confident that the final pieces of the puzzle will eventually fall into place.

• TREATMENT FOR •

Hallucinatory Behaviors

The most prevalent hallucinatory behaviors involve chasing lights or shadows or snapping at imaginary flies.

Diagnosis

1. Purely by observation and quantitation of the behavior (same criteria apply as for Bull Terriers—see summary at the end of chapter 11)
2. EEG may be useful to elucidate possible underlying seizure activity
3. CT scan, MRI or PET/SPECT scanning may be helpful in the future

Treatment

1. Enrich the dog's environment, making it as diverse and interesting as possible. Minimize the use of a crate and other forms of confinement, and minimize the time the dog spends alone.
2. Provide an appropriate diet and adequate exercise.
3. Try withdrawing your attention when the dog actively engages in this behavior. A bridging stimulus can be useful in this context.
4. Medication (anticonvulsants and/or antiobsessional drugs) may be prescribed by a veterinarian.

CHAPTER 13

Licking a Problem

I t was 1989 when I first met Taylor, a three-year-old red Doberman from Springfield, Massachusetts. Very handsome and an
extremely good example of the breed, Taylor was shown and
used for stud. Unfortunately, this dog, like many Dobermans, had a
licking problem. Taylor was first noticed to be somewhat orally
inclined when he was about one month of age; he would knead
cushions and blankets with his paws, mouthing and sucking the
items until they were wet. Taylor had been orphaned as a pup and
hand-reared from birth, so this appeared to be displaced nursing
behavior, akin to human thumb-sucking. As a puppy would also
nurse on other dogs' ears, and when there were no blankets or ears
around, he would just suck and chew stones or mouth the skin of
his flank until it was moist with saliva. Blanket sucking and flank
sucking occur almost exclusively in Dobermans, suggesting that the

condition may be genetic. In Taylor's case, however, it was hard to resist the explanation that the behavior was a result of maternal deprivation. Most likely, though, complex behaviors such as compulsive licking arise from a combination of nature and nuture, both components being necessary for the full expression of the condition. Freud would probably have been intrigued by Taylor's behavior and would have had no hesitation in branding him an oral retentive.

When Taylor was two, he started another oral activity: licking his legs. First it was the lower extremity of his right hind leg, and then he shifted his attention to his right wrist. He also started to lick and chew his right flank with greater intensity than he had previously. By the time I saw him, he had turned most of his attention to his left wrist, although his flank was still a major preoccupation and he had licked and chewed it so much that it had become a large, festering sore. His left wrist was none too pretty, either, sporting a round, raised, ulcerated area about the size of a quarter. Taylor's owner, Pam Rhodes, was a charming and intelligent woman who was apparently quite well known in Doberman breeding circles. She was very concerned about Taylor's condition, not only because he looked dreadful and could not be shown, but also because she was worried about his health.

I explained to Pam that this condition might result from both genetic factors and environmental influences (the latter particularly during the critical first three months of life). I also discussed the role of boredom or stress as a promoter of the condition. It is widely held that excessive localized licking of the extremities, resulting in what are called lick granulomas, is a condition that arises from stress or the boredom of confinement. Typically, owners of affected dogs report that their pet is left on its own for several hours a day. When a bored dog grooms a conveniently situated region of its body (say, a forelimb when the dog is lying down on its chest or flank, or a hind limb when the dog is curled around and lying on its side), the activity is thought to afford some sort of relief from the boredom or stress, and the behavior may become self-reinforcing. Grooming as a displacement behavior then assumes a new dimension. With time, the licking causes erosion of the skin and the formation of a granuloma (a mass of chronically inflamed tissue). The licking behavior eventually becomes so ingrained that it is performed at any time, even when the dog is not alone and bored. At this point, when the neural pathways are well-worn and the behavior is automatic, it is referred to as a stereotypy. The dictionary definition of a stereotypy is a behavior that is repetitive in form and, to the onlooker, apparently pointless and mindless. This kind of licking certainly fits the bill.

Pam listened to all these theories and explanations and admitted that Taylor was left alone for several hours a day when he wasn't being worked. She also recognized that the behavior had now assumed the proportions of a stereotypy and acknowledged that no amount of veterinary treatment had made the slightest bit of difference in the behavior. Her local veterinarian had tried applying various potions and balms to the leg itself and had tried bandaging the lesion so that Taylor could not get at it. At one point, they had even put a large, cone-shaped plastic collar around the dog's neck to physically prevent him from getting at the limb. As long as he couldn't get at it, the sore would start to heal, but he couldn't live in the plastic collar forever, and as soon as the device was removed he would get right back to licking his leg again and reopen the wound.

I discussed some treatment alternatives with Pam, starting with some potentially beneficial ways of modifying Taylor's management and environment. First, I explained that exercise would be beneficial for Taylor's condition. As it was, he was getting very little. Exercise would help to get rid of surplus energy and prevent unwanted behaviors. I recommended that she exercise Taylor for twenty to thirty minutes each day and that the exercise should be aerobic, not simply a walk. I also gave Pam some advice about Taylor's diet and recommended that since he led a fairly sedentary life, he might benefit from a low-energy diet, possibly some kind of geriatric ration.

In terms of specific behavior-modification therapy, I advised Pam to enrich Taylor's environment, providing distractions for him at times when he would otherwise be bored and have nothing to do. It is easy to accomplish this when owners are around, utilizing components of obedience training, interactive activities such as grooming, and games, but to provide entertainment for a dog in the owners' absence is somewhat more challenging. Over the years, I have contrived a number of ways of providing dogs with entertainment in their owners' absence, and most of these involve providing a selection of novel play toys and long-lasting food treats, which are rotated to maintain the dog's interest. I asked Pam to leave Taylor hollow bones or Kong toys stuffed with peanut butter when she went out. In addition, though it was a long shot, I mentioned the possible benefits of playing recorded household sounds, including human voices, on a tape loop. Pam listened carefully to all I had to say, but before I began to discuss the medical side of treatment, she asked the $64,000 question: "If I carry out all these suggestions, what's the likelihood that the licking will stop completely?"

"Not good," I was forced to reply, "but without environmental enrichment and changes in Taylor's management, the pharmacological treatment that I am about to suggest will be less likely to succeed."

I proceeded to discuss a new drug treatment that I developed at Tufts along with Dr. Lou Shuster. In essence, I explained, stress releases certain brain chemicals, or neurotransmitters, called endorphins. Endorphins then activate another neurotransmitter, called dopamine, which connects thought with action. Too little dopamine results in movement disorders, like Parkinson's disease. Too much causes hyperactivity and stereotypy—Taylor's problem. If the endorphins were blocked, as with this drug, then the stereotypic licking should decrease or cease altogether.

"Are endorphins the chemicals that create what's called runner's high?" Pam asked.

"They are," I confirmed. "I have often wondered if the activity of self-grooming feeds back to cause even more endorphin release, creating a sort of vicious circle. If this was the case, affected dogs could even be achieving a sort of licker's high!"

Pam nodded slowly and then turned to Taylor. "You're a good boy," I heard her say, almost under her breath. Taylor sat at her side looking on patiently, almost wisely, as if he understood what was being said.

Pam agreed to medicate Taylor for a trial period. Our interview concluded, and the two of them departed the clinic after a brief visit to the pharmacy to pick up the medication.

I didn't speak to Pam again for a couple of weeks. When we next talked, she reported a 50 percent decrease in the licking behavior. I advised her to increase the dose and keep medicating Taylor for a while longer. This she did, and three weeks later she jubilantly informed me that the behavior had stopped completely the day after I asked her to increase the dose. Not only had Taylor stopped licking his leg, but he had also stopped licking his flank and stopped chewing stones! Pam was delighted, and, I must admit, so was I. Although I had seen the licking stop for a short while following a test injection of the endorphin-blocking drug, Taylor was my first clinical success using the oral form of the medication. I weaned Taylor off the medication over the course of a week or two and the licking behavior did not start again . . . at least for a while. It appeared that Taylor was completely cured, and the lesions began to heal. Some months later, he looked so good that Pam even entered him in a show.

Taylor did have a couple of flare-ups later on, at about six-month intervals. Each one was precipitated by an incident of minor trauma. One time he was nipped by another dog, and on another occasion he was bitten by an insect. Both of these events caused him to lick the affected area furiously, and after a while it appeared to Pam that he was getting back into the rhythmic licking mode that had caused the trouble before. On each occasion, I instituted a short course of medication, and the behavior resolved within a week or two. I found myself explaining the relapses to Pam using the analogy of a swinging pendulum. Like a pendulum, the licking behavior, once arrested, would remain quiescent until activated by some stimulus. When initiated, however, the behavior would continue until arrested again. With the problem controlled like this, Taylor lived happily for several years during which I maintained close contact with him through Pam.

Around the time of my treatment success with Taylor, I was called up by a dermatologist from the Mayo Clinic. He had read some publications that Dr. Lou Shuster and I had written regarding endorphin-blocking drugs for the treatment of lick granuloma in dogs and cribbing in horses and was interested to know whether I thought these medications would be useful for one of his human patients. The patient was described to me as a middle-aged man, the vice president of a major U.S. corporation, who had begun to scratch and pick at the side of his face some years before (this is called neurotic excoriation). The man had continued the behavior to the point where his face was ulcerated and bleeding most of the time. He had seriously damaged the nostril on one side of his face and had gouged the temporal area of his forehead. It seems he just couldn't stop himself. The behavior had caused serious and unsightly injuries and was distressing to him. No treatment the doctors had tried had been more than temporarily successful, and the possibility of trying endorphin-blocking drugs was one of the few options left open to them. I provided them with some information about dosages in humans and informed them that I thought the medication would be worth a try. As it turns out, the results of the trial were even more spectacular with this man than with Taylor. He stopped scratching and picking at his face within three days of the first oral dose of medication, and during one month of treatment left his face alone so that the lesions began to heal. When the medicine was stopped, this man, like Taylor, did not start the behavior again, and six weeks later his face was almost completely healed. The doctors at the Mayo Clinic were so impressed by their success that they wrote a letter to the editor of a prestigious dermatology journal to share the results with their colleagues. I thought about calling up the patient to ask if he was interested in sponsoring some further studies in dogs, but then I thought better of it— he probably would not have been pleased to learn that his treatment was prescribed by a vet.

An endorphin-blocking drug has recently been introduced for the treatment of alcoholism. This implies that similar reward mechanisms may be operating to reinforce the craving for alcohol as are operating in neurotic excoriation and canine compulsive licking. Not all the dogs with lick granuloma that I have treated with endorphin-blocking drugs have responded well, however. The reason for this is not clear to me at present. I can only suggest that there may be different types of licking problems with different mechanisms operating.

In 1990 one of the veterinary journals published an important article describing the successful treatment of canine lick granuloma with a human antiobsessional drug, Anafranil. Anafranil, like Prozac, makes the neurotransmitter serotonin more available in the brain by blocking its reabsorption once it is secreted. Serotonin is, among other things, involved in the regulation of mood, and, in general, higher and more consistent levels of serotonin have a stabilizing effect on mood. Because dogs with lick granuloma responded to Anafranil and because of the similarities between compulsive paw licking in dogs and compulsive hand washing in people, the authors of the article felt that lick granuloma was the canine equivalent of human obsessive-compulsive disorder (OCD). About 85 percent of cases of OCD in people involve a preoccupation with cleanliness, germs, and disease, leading to the compulsive washing and cleaning rituals. This poses a problem when we try to use human OCD as a model for dogs, because animals have no conception of germs or disease prevention. But children, who are also uninitiated in these matters, can develop obsessions about things that look like contaminants but really are not, such as the color blue, or may even develop compulsions *without* a preceding obsession. Perhaps affected dogs are more like children in this respect, having primary compulsions preceded at best by rudimentary obsessions ("This grooming job just needs a few more licks").

One of the first dogs that I treated with antiobsessional medication was a rather large and wooly black mixed-breed dog called Stan. Luckily for me, Stan's owner was a psychologist with a Ph.D. and was familiar with obsessive-compulsive disorder and its treatment. I could tell right away that Stan was very important to her and that she would leave no stone unturned to help him. In this instance, I was particularly grateful to be dealing with an educated client who had the determination and financial resources to allow me to treat Stan appropriately. Stan's lick granuloma was one of the worst I have seen. It was so deeply ulcerated that I was concerned that the underlying bone might become infected, though I refrained from telling Stan's worried owner about a case I heard of in which a bone infection that resulted from a lick granuloma had necessitated amputation of the affected limb. Anyway, Stan was medicated with Anafranil, and I stayed in touch with his owner as the weeks ticked by. The results of the treatment were most impressive. Stan gradually stopped licking over about three months of treatment, and his recovery followed the same kind of pattern as that of human OCD patients when treated this way. After two weeks, he was 50 percent better; after four weeks, he was 75 percent better, and so on, until eventually the lesion was almost completely healed and licking was occasional and desultory. We never quite achieved a 100 percent cure, but the success was nevertheless remarkable, and Stan's owner remains thankful to this day. Stan is still on treatment as I write this, some two years later, and it seems that old age will catch up with him before the lick granuloma does.

There are many other repetitive behaviors that dogs exhibit that are currently referred to as stereotypy *or* obsessive-compulsive disorder, depending on which school of thought you choose to follow. I have had cases where dogs lick the floor obsessively or lick varnished wood surfaces. Some of them lick so constantly that they leave deep impressions in rugs or completely remove the varnish from lacquered surfaces. Cocker Spaniels seem to be over-represented among the varnish lickers, leading me to suspect an underlying genetic component. If this was substantiated, it would lend support to the obsessive-compulsive disorder theory. Lick granuloma itself appears to be familial and is common in larger breeds, such as Dobermans, Labradors, and other retrievers. As dis-cussed in the preceding chapter, some dogs indulge in different repetitive behaviors such as snapping at imaginary flies or chasing shadows, while others seem to be constantly looking for something that isn't there or chase their tail until they collapse from exhaus-tion. We still don't know exactly what is going on in all these cases, but they too may be forms of obsessive-compulsive disorder. If antiobsessional drugs prove effective against a particular repetitive condition, that tilts the balance in favor of a diagnosis of OCD. Studies of these problems are ongoing in our clinic and at other veterinary schools.

• TREATMENT FOR •

Lick Granuloma

This condition is characterized by repetitive licking directed at one spot, often on the lower extremity of the limbs. Attention may shift from one location to another over time. Large breeds of dog (Labrador Retriever, German Shepherd, Great Dane, Doberman) are primarily affected. Affected dogs are often high-strung or have an anxious temperament.

Treatment

1. It is best to choose a diet that is appropriate for your dog's level of activity—for example, avoid high-performance food for a house pet that spends most of its time confined or resting.
2. The more exercise that you can provide, the better. Twenty to thirty minutes of aerobic exercise per day is the bare minimum.
3. Provide a diverse and interesting environment, with plenty of mobile and chewable toys.
4. Antibiotics should be prescribed by your veterinarian if infection is present.
5. Medication with an antiobsessional drug, such as Prozac (fluoxetine) or Anafranil (clomipramine) may be appropriate. Alternatively, opioid antagonists, like naltrexone may bring about dramatic improvements.

CHAPTER 14

To Pee or Not to Pee

I must admit that when I started seeing canine problem-behavior cases, I wasn't enthusiastic about tackling the problem of inappropriate elimination of urine and feces (as it is euphemistically called). I was able to avoid this issue for some time, dismissing it as a rather dull and uninteresting training problem of minor importance. How wrong I was! First of all, inappropriate-elimination problems present a diagnostic and therapeutic challenge. Second, failure to correct this sometimes refractory problem can have dire consequences for the pet. Dogs, like many other species, are inherently clean creatures. They have an inborn tendency to void urine and feces at sites remote from their dining and sleeping areas. This apparent fastidiousness may exist because it confers an evolutionary edge: clean dogs are less likely to pick up parasites. Why, then, is inappropriate elimination in the home one of the most common canine behavior problems, by some estimates constituting ten to twenty percent of cases? And why do some people have such difficulty training (or retraining) their dogs to eliminate in the great outdoors that the problem assumes life-threatening proportions for the pet? Sadly, a large number of the hundreds of thousands of dogs that meet their untimely demise at the hands of the authorities each month have inappropriate-elimination problems underlying their surrender to the pound or shelter. Many of these dogs have owners who love them but can no longer take the pressure of cohabiting with a house-soiling pet.

The first and most obvious explanation for house-soiling problems is that many dogs are not free to leave the house at will and sometimes have no option but to foul the nest. This is particularly likely when young pups are left for extended periods of time, because they require frequent pit stops. A rule of thumb is that a puppy can hold its urine for the number of hours that corresponds to its age in months plus one. By the time a dog has reached young adulthood, it can go eight to ten hours without having to go out, depending on the amount of water it has consumed.

In attempting to understand elimination problems, it is imperative to remember that urination and defecation are more for the dog than just the excretion of bodily wastes. As odd as it may seem to us, the deposition of urine and feces is also a means of visual and olfactory communication. Timid dogs squat and urinate to signal deference, while dominant dogs mark everything in sight to claim it as their own. The "Kilroy was here" message is encoded in biological scent markers called pheromones, which are the canine equivalent of calling cards. Full-grown unneutered males are the most prolific at this marking game, driven by their hormones. Other nonexcretory causes of inappropriate urination include medical problems, such as cystitis, and extreme fear and anxiety. Deciding what the real problem is can sometimes be a bit of a puzzle.

One spring day I had a visit from a delightful client, Charlotte Arnold, and her recently acquired Wire-Haired Fox Terrier, Bushka. I had seen Charlotte before regarding her previous dog, a Welsh Corgi that had been giving her some problems related to dominance. Charlotte, a retired schoolteacher, had obtained Bushka from a pound about eight months earlier to fill the void created by the loss of her old companion. It wasn't long before she realized why the dog's previous owners had parted with her. Bushka was an incorrigible house soiler, urinating all over the place up to eight times daily. To make matters worse, she would also occasionally defecate on the kitchen floor. Charlotte had been told that one of the reasons for Bushka's urinary incontinence problem was that she had a "pelvic bladder"—a bladder that was too small to hold an adequate volume of urine. Maybe, maybe not. But the problem—whatever was causing it—was driving Charlotte to distraction.

By the time I saw Bushka, she had already undergone surgery for the so-called pelvic bladder, and Charlotte reported that, if anything, the problem was slightly worse. When inappropriate defecation accompanies inappropriate urination, I am always inclined to think of a house-training problem rather than a medical problem. Nevertheless, I reviewed Bushka's medical records first, paying particular attention to the most recent results of blood and urine analyses, although I didn't really expect to find anything significant. After ruling out medical problems as well as I could, I decided to treat Bushka as if she had suffered a breakdown in her house-training routine.

I told Charlotte to escort Bushka on lead to a convenient location outside the house several times a day and to give her sufficient time, say fifteen minutes, to produce the desired result. In order to make the chosen site more attractive, Charlotte was advised to lay urine-soaked newspaper in the area to provide Bushka with the correct olfactory cues for elimination. The timing of excursions to the site was to be as follows: first thing in the morning, at three-hour intervals during the day, and last thing at night. In addition, Charlotte was to take Bushka out fifteen or twenty minutes after eating and immediately after napping, chewing, or playing. Charlotte was instructed to walk Bushka briskly to and from the site, not allowing her to become distracted from the task at hand. The whole sequence should be paired with some auditory cue, such as the "Hurry up" phrase popularized by the late Barbara Woodhouse. If Bushka performed on cue, she was to be praised immediately and given a highly palatable food treat, such as freeze-dried liver, to reward and reinforce the behavior. I explained that rewarding Bushka more than a few seconds after the happy event might reinforce the wrong behavior, such as gazing at a bird in a nearby tree, so timing was critical. On successful completion of a mission, Bushka would be allowed back in the house in a restricted area under direct supervision. In the event that Bushka exhibited any signs of impending urination, such as circling, sniffing the ground, or simply appearing restless, she was to be taken out again immediately and encouraged to use the proper site. If Bushka *did not* urinate or defecate when taken outside, she was to be brought back inside and confined in a smallish area, perhaps a crate, for fifteen minutes before being taken out again. As Bushka was already acclimated to a crate, I thought this would be a particularly useful, nonstressful place for her to be confined.

Most dogs will not urinate inside a crate, providing it is small enough, as they will not be able to escape from the mess. They will usually hang on as long as they can, waiting for a better opportunity. Crates may not work to discourage urination in dogs that have been confined for so long that they have been compelled to eliminate there against their better judgment. In such cases, the cleanliness code is broken and subsequent confinement is no safeguard. Very small dogs in a large crate can simply move to the other end and get away from the mess. Crates should be long enough for dogs to lie down comfortably, wide enough for them to turn around, and tall enough for them to stand—in other words, they should be snug. Some dogs become hysterical if crated, especially if they have not been conditioned to regard the crate as the safe haven (or den) it should represent. Dogs with a dislike of their crate may be reacclimated over several weeks by feeding them close to and finally in the crate and by rewarding them with food treats, petting, and praise for entering the open crate. Using confinement to a crate as a punishment is counterproductive to establishing the idea that the crate is a den or sanctuary.

Bushka did have a bit of a crate problem; she would occasionally urinate on her blanket in the crate when she was confined at night. When this happened, Charlotte would find the blanket pushed up into a wet heap at the far end of the crate. I thought that the absorbent properties of the blanket might be allowing Bushka to urinate without dirtying the crate, and so I advised Charlotte to remove it for a time to see if this would encourage Bushka to hang on a bit longer. Just in case we were unable to use the crate effectively in the retraining process, I mentioned other confinement options that Charlotte might have to resort to. These included tying Bushka to the kitchen table leg on a short lead between trips to the yard or the use of what is called umbilical cord training, in which

Charlotte would attach Bushka's lead to her belt and have her around her feet all day long while she was at home. Whatever the method of confinement or restriction, the general principal utilized is the same: that a dog will generally not urinate or defecate where it stands due to its inborn cleanliness instincts.

Charlotte understood all that had to be done regarding training, but she did have a question, and it was a good one.

"What do I do if Bushka starts to urinate right in front of me and I am unable to get to her in time? Should I scold her or simply ignore it?" she queried.

"Don't scold her," I replied. "If you do, she'll just go when you're not looking and will be reluctant to urinate in front of you when you take her out. You *can* make a sudden noise, however, such as banging on the table or shaking a can with pennies inside. A sudden rude interruption like that will shut down her sphincters and cut her off in midstream. You should then swiftly attach her lead, take her out, and clean up the mess later."

Charlotte understood everything I had told her, so I proceeded with another important aspect in the control of house soiling: cleanup.

"It is absolutely imperative," I told Charlotte, "that you clean up every mess, because the odors will attract Bushka back to the same spot as surely as a source of heat attracts a heat-seeking missile. In addition to soaking up the urine with paper towels and cleaning the soiled area with soap and water, you must treat these areas with a professionally manufactured odor neutralizer. Trying to mask the odor with vinegar or ammonia just won't do, so don't even bother trying. Odor neutralizers actually destroy the source of the odor, and that's what you have to do. There are basically two different types of neutralizer, those containing enzymes and those containing bacteria, and they're about equally effective. Because they are biological, both products are sensitive to chemicals and extremes of temperature, so they have to be treated carefully if they are to remain effective. Don't leave them out in a warm, sunny place, and don't treat a soiled area with bleach first and then expect the odor neutralizer to work."

Charlotte set off to give the program a try. As requested, she called me back a week later for follow-up. There had been great improvement in Bushka's condition. She had taken to the new routine like a duck to water and was now effectively housebroken—at least during the daytime. In fact, there had been *no* daytime incidents of inappropriate elimination since our consultation . . . but nighttime was another matter. At about four-thirty or five in the morning, Bushka would start to bark incessantly. Charlotte would then have to get up pretty quickly to take her out or Bushka would have an accident in the crate. It seemed that removing the blanket from the crate was working, because Bushka had never complained like this before—she had just urinated on the blanket and gone back to sleep. It was possible to maintain Bushka accident-free for the entire twenty-four-hour period, but the prospect of getting up at four-thirty every day for the rest of her life was causing Charlotte considerable anguish. I wondered whether the problem might have something to do with her small bladder, which limited her ability to hold urine, and Charlotte admitted that she had never known Bushka to go for longer than four to six hours without urinating. But Charlotte also told me that she was walking around in a fog all day because of lack of sleep and was experiencing great difficulties meeting her many obligations. I had to do something else, but what?

I cast my mind back to a time when one of my kids had a

problem getting through the night without a pit stop, resulting in bed-wetting incidents at an age when these should have been history. At that time, I looked into the medical basis of the condition (termed enuresis) and its treatment. One of the options was to prescribe a tricyclic antidepressant that, among other things, increases tone in the sphincter muscle at the neck of the bladder. Armed with this knowledge and some familiarity with the use of these drugs in dogs, I advised Charlotte to try Bushka on one of these medications, Tofranil. The results were quick and dramatic. A single small daily dose enabled Bushka (and hence Charlotte) to get through the entire night. At last report, Bushka was still taking this innocuous (and relatively inexpensive) medication, and was maintaining her accident-free record.

I was extremely pleased to have been able to solve this problem for Charlotte, not only because it was a challenge, but also because I felt that Charlotte was close to bringing Bushka back to the pound. That would certainly have been the end of the road for her this time. Although Charlotte was an extremely compassionate and dedicated owner, her nerves had been frayed by eight months of unsuccessful efforts prior to her visit to Tufts, and she was at the end of her tether. I realized from the outset that any treatment I devised was a last-ditch effort.

Bushka's house-soiling problem was fairly classic and probably stemmed from earlier ineffective house-training methods; perhaps it had been exacerbated by her stay in the pound. Certainly her crate-wetting was an indication of lack of attention at some point in her life. Another factor that was stacked against her was genetics. Terriers in general seem to be a bit of a challenge to housebreak properly, especially if there is more than one dog in the household. When people call me up and report a house-soiling problem in a terrier, I am tempted to gravitate immediately to a diagnosis of ineffective house-training. On one occasion, however, I fell afoul of my own prejudices and managed to solve the problem only after some not-too-clever backpedaling. The owner in question had two Yorkshire Terriers, one of which had been urinating in the house for more than a year. Without subjecting her dog to a battery of tests, I attempted to work with a retraining program from the outset, but after two weeks there was little change in the behavior. At this point, I did what I should have done in the first place. I took a urine sample and sent it to the laboratory for biochemical analysis, a bacterial culture, and antibiotic sensitivity. As it turned out, the dog had low-grade cystitis that responded almost immediately to a three-week course of an appropriate antibiotic. The client was inconvenienced by my oversight, but was contented by the eventual resolution of the problem. The experience I gained from my omission was invaluable. I now test for medical conditions in every case, however obvious the problem may appear, and do not intend to make that mistake again.

Many other medical conditions, ranging from kidney disease and endocrine disorders to a sort of canine Alzheimer's disease, may be associated with inappropriate urination. Some older dogs with incontinence problems have what is called cognitive dysfunction syndrome. Basically, affected dogs just lose urinary control as a result of changes that aging causes in the brain. Luckily, a new drug will soon be available for cognitive dysfunction syndrome, bringing new hope to the owners of elderly pets. Deprenyl works a bit like some of the earlier antidepressants, the monoamine oxidase inhibitors, but it does not interact with certain foods the way MAOIs do, and so there is no adverse reaction if your dog partakes of a little cheese while on medication. Treated dogs may start to behave like youngsters, and there is some laboratory evidence of an enhanced life span. One owner reported that her ten-year-old Irish Setter, recently treated with Deprenyl, was suddenly behaving like a two-year-old. The veterinarian prescribing the medication interpreted this as good news—but the owner said that she hadn't liked the dog's behavior when it was two because at that age it had been hyperactive and generally a pain to live with. The dose of the medication was subsequently adjusted until the dog was behaving like a six-year-old!

Sometimes the cause of inappropriate urination is even more obvious than those mentioned already. For example, anyone who owns an unneutered male dog may well find that dog cocking its leg on the furniture, particularly if the dog has something to prove. Neighborhood bitches coming into heat can increase the frequency of this problem to mind-boggling proportions, as can the addition of new dogs to the household. This type of behavior is entirely normal and, from the dog's point of view, is far from inappropriate. In males it is hormonally driven to some extent and also seems to be related to dominance. The hallmark of this marking behavior is the depositing of small volumes of urine in strategic locations. It's known as the calling card syndrome—a form of canine graffiti. Luckily, most cases of leg lifting are easily controlled by neutering. Some 90 percent of dogs will cease the behavior within a few weeks of surgery. Of those that continue, many can be brought under control using dominance restructuring tactics, which center around rewarding submissive behavior.

The final category of inappropriate elimination falls under the general heading of anxiety or fear-induced elimination disorders. Stretching the definition a little, the type most frequently encountered is probably submissive urination. In this condition, a young dog, usually a female and usually between six months and two years of age, will urinate while greeting people at the door, or when spoken to or approached by certain people. Reaching for the dog's collar or putting on the dog's lead are actions that frequently initiate this behavior. Dogs that signal this way tend to be of a timid disposition and may have had their confidence shaken by firm treatment or militaristic obedience-training methods. Certain breeds, notably Cocker Spaniels, seem to be particularly prone to submissive urination. In susceptible dogs' eyes, the "challenger" is so overwhelming that the dog feels compelled to perform a submissive gesture of respect—namely, squatting and urinating, or rolling over. Men, on account of their physical attributes (stature, voice, body language), are particularly likely to inspire this type of behavior in susceptible dogs. Submissive urination is really an extreme compliment, but it is hard to see this as urine soaks into your best rug or seeps under your shoes. It is easy to understand why some people yell at their dogs for doing this, but alas, such a response has exactly the opposite effect. The dog feels that it has not been humble enough and proceeds to squat even lower and urinate again. The only way to deal with these cases is to back off. The more active you become in trying to address this problem, the worse it becomes.

The most recent case of submissive urination I dealt with involved a young pup that belonged to one of our equine-ward attendants, Will. The pup, called Misty, was a six-month-old female Cocker Spaniel. I advised Will to enter his home without looking at or speaking to the pup and to take a detour directly to the kitchen and get himself seated. He was also instructed to back off on obedience training and to encourage dominance by applying a dominance-management program in reverse. One key component of this program was for Will to play tug-of-war with the pup each night *and to let the dog win.* Also, when addressing Misty in the home or when putting on the lead (a serious problem area in this case), I advised him to crouch on one knee and call the dog to him rather than to approach her and loom over her. Will followed this advice and things improved considerably, although the pup still urinated every time he went to put on the lead. This last problem area proved extremely difficult to deal with despite Will's valiant efforts. What else could I advise? Then it came to me—he should not be facing the dog at all during this interaction. Consequently, I had him approach Misty by crouching down and shuffling toward her backside first, attaching the lead by fumbling around behind himself. We both hoped his neighbors would not look through the windows at these times and figure he needed psychiatric help . . . but however odd and embarrassing the plan was, it worked! Even better from Will's perspective, after a few weeks he was able to quit shuffling around on the floor, and Misty didn't resume the submissive urination. She had learned it wasn't necessary. Most dogs eventually grow out of this problem as they gain confidence and grow to adulthood, but six to twelve months of wet rugs can be a real pain, so behavior modification is usually welcomed. I view the restructuring of interactions as a way of expediting the natural course of events.

Other anxiety-related elimination problems can be a little more insidious than submissive urination. Urination associated with separation anxiety falls into this category. The diagnosis is usually fairly simple, as the urination (and/or defecation) occurs only when the owner is away. Dogs affected with separation anxiety will be showing many of the other telltale signs, too, including following the owner around the house, displaying signs of anxiety when the owner prepares to depart, whimpering or barking after the owner has left, temporary (psychogenic) anorexia, destructive behavior during the owner's absence, and exuberant greeting behavior on the owner's return. In these latter cases, treatment of the separation anxiety is all that is required for the inappropriate elimination behavior to cease.

One last type of anxiety-related inappropriate elimination relates to the anxiety created by changes in the structure of the household. One such case I recall was reported in a four-year-old female Lhasa Apso called Maxine. This dog's owner reported that the elimination problem started the day she brought her new baby home from the hospital. Maxine started urinating and defecating, apparently indiscriminately, on the carpeted floor. This anxiety-related marking behavior was compounded by the owners, who became extremely irritated and started yelling when they caught Maxine in the act. The behavior was thus reinforced as a way for the dog to get the attention she wanted. The advice given to these owners was to pay more attention to Maxine when the baby was around and to pay little attention to her at other times. They were also told to deal with inappropriate-elimination events calmly and to use an odor neutralizer to treat soiled areas. Maxine was given a mild anxiety-reducing drug, buspirone, to help her to cope with the new challenge, and the rest was just a matter of time. On follow-up one month later, Maxine was reported to be calmer and "more loveable," and there had been only one inappropriate-elimination incident in the entire period. Following this, even when the medication was discontinued, there were no more accidents, and I was able to log the problem as successfully resolved.

Since the early days I have gained a better understanding of the importance of making an accurate diagnosis when treating inappropriate-elimination disorders. In this context, I have realized that performing a thorough physical examination of the animal, including appropriate laboratory tests, and obtaining a detailed behavioral history are of paramount importance. With the diagnosis made, the treatment is usually fairly straightforward. I am happy to report that I have been able to treat successfully almost all of the patients I have been presented with in recent years, including one case in which an eight-year-old Bichon Frise had been urinating and defecating in the house for its entire life. Although this dog would urinate in a crate, it had never urinated in the owner's bedroom, so that was used as a place of confinement during the retraining process. Both the owner and I were amazed at how rapidly successful the retraining process was. If I could retrain that dog, I told myself, I am ready for any waterworks problem.

• TREATMENT FOR •

Inappropriate Elimination

In the majority of cases, urination and defecation by dogs within the home is a normal (for the dog) behavior usually caused by ineffective house-training methods, particularly in young dogs. Another reason for inappropriate elimination is marking, which is particularly pronounced in dominant male dogs, where it takes the form of leg lifting. There are also medical causes of inappropriate elimination, particularly in older dogs. Dogs that urinate or defecate *only* when their owners are away may have separation anxiety.

Treatment

1. For inappropriate elimination resulting from inadequate house-training, retraining the dog to a particular location outside the home may be all that is necessary.
2. For treatment of marking behaviors in adult male dogs, neutering must be considered the treatment of choice when this is an option. For other types of marking behavior, dominance restructuring or antianxiety medication can be helpful.
3. Treat anxiety-based conditions by attempting to reduce the cause of the anxiety. Medication—for example, buspirone—can be useful.
4. Medical conditions should be diagnosed and treated first by your local veterinarian if there is any suspicion of their involvement.

Epilogue

The cases referred to in this book provide a cross-section of some of the most important behavior problems encountered in dogs and indicate some solutions to these problems. The causes of canine behavior problems are important to understand because understanding them paves the way for the best solution of all: prevention. Some conditions have a large genetic component that is subsequently fueled by environmental pressures and experiences. In other cases, an otherwise well-balanced dog can develop a behavior problem as a result of adverse environmental experiences that tax its endurance beyond reasonable limits. The unscrupulous breeding of pedigree dogs for conformation only, with no attempt to select for an even temperament, has led to many suspect lines in certain breeds, particularly with regard to aggression. This matter has been discussed in detail in *Time* magazine and also on the television program *20/20*. As one trainer remarked on the show, "They're breeding garbage." This statement certainly makes the point, and many of us are left wondering whether ethical breeding practices have literally gone to the dogs or whether breed clubs will wake up in time to address this vital issue.

Another complicating factor is that a number of television shows have popularized some of the dog breeds known for negative behaviors—which, of course, aren't shown on TV. It is always a great surprise to people who buy a Jack Russell Terrier because they fell in love with Eddie, a Jack Russell Terrier on the television show *Frasier,* to find out that the dog is, after all, a terrier, with tendencies to be yappy, hyperactive, and even nippy; certainly no angel. The Disney movie *101 Dalmatians* popularized the Dalmatian, a dog originally bred in the 1800s for guarding carriages. The Dalmatian's guarding tendencies stem from dominance and protectiveness. This hidden side of their personality is contrary to the expectations of young film-goers who imagine that all dogs of this breed are lovable and friendly, just like their Disney caricatures. Then there are the dogs featured in *Lady and the Tramp* and *Beethoven* as well as Spuds MacKenzie, the dog we all know from beer commercials. The bottom line is that none of these breeds is fundamentally bad, but each has its own behavioral idiosyncracies, and some of these character quirks may not fit in with a would-be owner's lifestyle or personality. Certain specialized breeds, such as Rottweilers and Akitas, require prior knowledge of dog handling for successful management. These are not breeds for the novice owner. In addition to breed genetics, it is also advisable to check out the family line too, although it is sometimes difficult to get straight answers to probing questions from breeders. Meeting the bitch and sire can help put your mind at ease about these close relatives and provide some additional security. They should be happy-go-lucky and pettable; neither should they growl at you, bark at you, or back away sheepishly. If you are discouraged from visiting with one or the other parent, this is usually a bad sign.

Some people may visit the pet store to pick up a book on dogs and find out something about the breeds they're interested in. But this doesn't work either, because the sections in the A to Z of dogs are often written by breeders who haven't got a bad word to say about their own specialty. Having people like them report on the dog's bad traits is like expecting a mother to report negatively about the intelligence or behavior of her own children. There are, however, a couple of good sources of information. I would recommend *Harper's Guide to Dogs,* edited by Roger Caras, or *Selecting a Puppy,* by Drs. Ben and Lynette Hart. These two books do provide an accurate and honest description of different breeds and show them in their true colors for their strengths and weaknesses.

I would strongly suggest that anybody who is about to purchase a new dog think seriously about the temperament and manageability of the breed they are planning to acquire, as well as other factors, such as coat length, expense of upkeep, grooming requirements, exercise requirements, suitability for their lifestyle, and environment. They should choose a dog that is appropriate for them, with or without the help of a trainer or behaviorist, because, after all, assuming things work out well, they will be spending fourteen to sixteen years with the pet they choose. It is a decision that should not be made on the spur of the moment or for cosmetic reasons, but rather is one that needs to be carefully thought out.

Assuming that an owner-to-be homes in on a suitable breed, the next question is: What age is optimal for the chances of behavior problems to be minimized? I recommend that dogs should be adopted at six to eight weeks of age. Anything earlier than this can lead to problems with undersocialization with other dogs, and anything older than this means that you are inheriting a black box of uncertainty. Perhaps it's okay if you know that the dog came from a good home, was well integrated with the family, and is properly socialized, but in many instances this is not the case. Even pound dogs can turn out fine if you know what to look for and what to avoid. Some of these poor animals can make very fine pets—and by acquiring one, you save a life. Whether you opt for a purebred pup or a pound dog, you should probably have a veterinarian's help in determining the temperament of that dog before you make your final commitment. Although puppy temperament evaluation is somewhat imprecise and scientists do not necessarily believe that this testing has any predictive power, the fact is that most dog professionals do acknowledge the efficacy of the technique. This test is usually conducted on the puppy's forty-ninth day (that is, when it is seven weeks old), but it may be necessary to test puppies more than once to make a valid prediction. I feel that, in the right hands, temperament testing is a useful practice that can provide valuable information about the dog you are about to acquire. Other factors may also give you a clue about the nature of a dog you are thinking of adopting. With pound dogs, certainly, you can predict potential problems with a reasonable degree of certainty. Separation anxiety, for example, can be predicted with nearly 100 percent accuracy.

What, then, do you do after you have acquired your dog? How should you proceed if it is a puppy? The answer is—as I've described in these pages—with a liberal dose of socialization. Puppy parties are a must. In addition, it is important to integrate the dog into the family unit and daily life. Do not park it in a kennel or anchor it to a tree. Work hard to achieve a high level of communication with the pet; provide plenty of exercise and entertainment for the dog; and, above all, be fair without spoiling or overindulging the new family member. Obedience training is also a helpful part of bringing up a dog, though this should not involve punitive measures but rather positive reinforcement that teaches it to respond to one-word commands. Setting limits is an important part of raising a socially compatible dog. Decide what behavior you desire from your dog and reward accordingly. As mentioned throughout the book, ignore all unwanted behavior.

If, despite all the above precautions, it becomes apparent that your dog is developing some behavior problem, try going back through the summaries at the end of each chapter or reread a relevant chapter to look for solutions. If the path to follow is not clear, seek additional help. The first place to call is probably your local veterinarian's office. Ask for some information on behavior and see if they can help. If not, ask if they can recommend a knowledgeable person to advise you regarding your dog's behavior problem. This person should preferably be an animal behaviorist or a veterinary behaviorist, although many trainers are experts in some of the management-related problems. Early intervention is best because it gives you a better chance of an effective cure. Once a behavior has become ingrained, it becomes much more difficult to turn it around. You certainly can teach old dogs new tricks; it just takes longer.

Following the guidelines described above, there is no reason why anyone should not have a well-balanced and friendly dog that is properly integrated into the family unit. Friends and family should be safe from unwanted aggressive outbursts, and the dog should be a good companion without being overly dependent. Fears and phobias can be prevented to some extent, and compulsive behaviors in susceptible dogs can be held at bay by proper management of the dog's lifestyle and environment. With proper selection, training, and management, and timely correction of unwanted behaviors, your dog can become a model canine citizen, and the bond that you develop and share can be strengthened.

About the Author

Nicholas H. Dodman is a veterinarian and director of the Animal Behavior Clinic at Tufts University School of Veterinary Medicine. He graduated from Glasgow University Veterinary School in 1970 and spent some years as a veterinary anesthesiologist before developing his now all-consuming interest in animal behavior. The transition from anesthesiologist to behaviorist was catalyzed by a remarkable discovery he made, along with his colleague Lou Shuster, that some repetitive behaviors in animals are fueled by nature's own morphine-like chemicals, the endorphins. This work led to the first of several U.S. patents that Dr. Dodman holds for ideas regarding behavioral physiology and pharmacology. Dr. Dodman, author of *Dogs Behaving Badly: An A to Z Guide to Understanding and Curing Behavioral Problems in Dogs,* is a nationally recognized leader and innovator in the field of domestic animal behavior. He has published over a hundred scientific articles on subjects ranging from veterinary anesthesiology and pharmacology to animal behavior, and is a board-certified member of the American College of Veterinary Behaviorists.

AND IF YOU THINK DOGS HAVE
PROBLEMS, WAIT UNTIL YOU READ
DR. DODMAN'S BOOK:

THE CAT WHO
CRIED FOR HELP

Attitudes, Emotions, and the Psychology of Cats

Dr. Nicholas Dodman turns his attention to
our feline friends in *The Cat Who Cried for
Help*, applying his cutting-edge treatments
and clever wit to the most common, and
most bizarre, cat psychological disorders.
You will never look at your cat the same way
after reading this book.

"*The Cat Who Cried for Help* establishes a
new frontier for the veterinary profession and
is essential reading for all who live with cats."
                                  Dr. Michael Fox

NFB 1 5/00